GO FOR IT!

GO FOR IT!

Dorothy R. Pape

WELCH PUBLISHING COMPANY INC.
Burlington, Ontario, Canada

ISBN:0-920413-92-7

© 1986 by Dorothy R. Pape

Welch Publishing Company Inc.
960 Gateway
Burlington, Ontario
L7L 5K7 Canada

Printed in Canada

CONTENTS

To Mary, his "thoroughbred," who was truly the helpmeet Hubert needed. Without her many letters to their prayer partners through the years this book could not have been written.

Chapter 1

FISH HOOKS FISHER

At the place where the Trans-Canada Highway crosses one of the most desolate, thickly wooded areas of its 4,000 mile length, only one sign greets travellers from east or west:

DON'T PICK UP HITCH-HIKERS:
THEY MAY BE ESCAPED PRISONERS

In woods to the south lies a small lake. Salmon and other excellent fish start life in its clean waters; then after two years growth they swim down river, drawn to the vaster depths of Lake Huron. Two years later, however, instinct urges them back to the lake of their birth for spawning.

But what difficulties this entails! They must fight their way upstream against strong currents; driftwood may batter them; rocks often tear their flesh. A twenty-pound salmon, a picture of determination, might hurl itself up a four-foot waterfall. But at last they can all find rest in that quiet lake hidden in the woods.

No sign pointed to the lake, however, nor was it advertised. For a mile from its shores lived a constantly changing group of men, who, unlike the fish, had mostly drifted with the current, perhaps because of bad companions, or perhaps through being too lazy to work, or keep the law. They were the inmates of a prison work camp. Most had not committed crimes of violence, but were here segregated from honest citizens, and employed in various forms of work.

One day in the early summer of 1924, a young man named Hubert Fisher arrived in the area to relieve the local railway station agent for a three-week holiday. Alighting from the train he noted with interest the surrounding country, for he hoped to be able to pursue his favorite sport of fishing while there.

The station agent introduced him to the various phases of the work; then shocked young Hubert with his next remark.

"It's tough cooking for yourself all the time. So I've arranged for you to have your meals at the prison camp from tomorrow.

They eat pretty well there. It's only a few minutes walk, and you can sleep on a cot in the guards' poolroom."

Hubert, or Bud as he was nicknamed, felt decidedly apprehensive as he went for his first meal with the prisoners. Glancing around the dining room he saw the majority were middle-aged men, though some were younger. It was a good dinner of roast pork, and most were too busy eating to talk. As they left the table, however, Bud put on his best smile, and looked for someone to speak to. Without introducing himself, a rather simple-looking youth nearby pointed to a plump, middle-aged man some yards away.

"Now there's a man that's got personality," he said, hero-worship shining in his eyes. "His name's Art—Art Dainty."

The man happened to turn towards them, and recognizing that Bud was a newcomer he came over. He also didn't bother to introduce himself, but launched into a lecture.

"Keep away from poolrooms, that's where young fellows go wrong. They get together in poolrooms and hatch up all kinds of mischief. I know. Many's the time I've seen it happen."

"I'm working at the railway station while the agent's on holiday. I'm just having my meals here," Bud hastily explained, thinking it wiser not to add he was to sleep in the poolroom.

"Well, take care you don't get into trouble then. I'm a trustee, and am in charge of the power-house at the lake which supplies the water for here. Come over sometime, and we'll go fishing."

Never one to refuse a fishing invitation, the minute his work was finished that afternoon Bud seized his line and spinner, and, full of anticipation, set off for the lake.

As he approached Art's cabin he saw an eight-foot fishing pole resting on two spikes above the door. There was no line, but a big triple hook, looking more like an anchor than a fishhook, was tied to the end of the pole.

"I haven't a pole, only a line and hook," he apologized as Art appeared at the door.

"I've a pole and hook, but no line," he answered, taking down his pole. Bud tied his line on just an inch from where the big hook was, and they set off down the narrow path to the lake, Art walking ahead with the pole.

The surroundings were beautiful, the only building in sight at the lake being the small red shack housing the pump which took water to the prison camp. The fresh green of early summer shrouded the maples and white birch, making them appear all the brighter against the darker pine and spruce. Such beauty was commonplace to Bud, however, and his mind was only on the big catch he hoped to make in this little-fished, unknown lake.

Art Dainty not only had "personality" but also an appreciation of his own importance and comfort. Accordingly, he stepped into the front of the boat with the fishing pole, and told Bud to do the paddling.

A strong wind blowing against them made paddling very hard work, but fortunately Art soon got a bite which nearly pulled the pole from his hands. Whatever was on the end of that line thrashed from side to side of the boat until finally the pole came over Bud's shoulder, and he felt a stabbing pain. That anchor-like hook had caught him!

"Just a minute, Art! Just a minute!" he shouted, rearing up. But Art was too engrossed holding onto the pole to notice.

In desperation Bud tried to step toward him, the paddle still in his hands. Art, used to handling prisoners and thinking Bud had gone crazy and was about to attack him with the paddle, hastily dropped the pole, and rolled over the side of the boat into the lake.

Just then the fish gave a great jerk which threw Bud off balance, and a second later, he, too, landed in the lake.

Seeing this, Art swam for shore as fast as he could, to escape this seeming madman.

Bud, meanwhile, noting the wind would blow the upturned boat safely to shore, concentrated on grabbing the pole and disentangling the hook from his shoulder. He hung on to the rod then, hoping to swim to shore with it. Sometimes the fish dragged him, and sometimes he succeeded in pulling the fish, until finally with a tremendous effort he reached shallow water.

Art was at the water's edge, wringing out his long woolen underwear. With aching arms, Bud finally reeled in the fish, and held it up for Art to see. It was a real beauty —a northern pike, nearly two feet long.

Art reached out to take it, but there was still some fight in that fish, and its teeth clamped down on Art's thumb. Blood began spurting onto his underwear, and by the time Bud managed to free the thumb the underwear was soaked in blood.

With a roar of disgust Art dumped the garment in the lake, and angrily indicated Bud should take the fish, and never come near him again.

In spite of his wonderful prize, it was a decidedly bedraggled and despondent Bud who walked back to the station, dripping water as he went. What a mess to get into! He had certainly lost Art as a friend. Besides, what on earth was he going to do with nearly 20 pounds of fish? How could he turn this embarrassing minus into a plus? As his mind pondered this problem an idea finally came. He could use this fish to make friends with the prisoners!

So, at midnight when the powerhouse gang at the camp changed crews, Bud, flashing his best smile, walked into the furnace room with the fish. A dozen men were there just beginning to eat, and one of them, the stoker, delightedly grabbed a poker, shoved it about a foot down through the fish's mouth, and stuck the fish into the furnace to bake.

The others expressed opinions as to whether it would be cooked yet or not, but the stoker ignored them. When it looked just right to him he pulled it out, and divided it among them all. The men shared their sandwiches with Bud, and all enjoyed a real feast.

"This man's a pretty good guy," whispered one of the men to the stoker. "Let's get him in our gang before any of the others ask him."

So the stoker shuffled over to Bud. "Will you join our baseball team?" he asked. "We need a pitcher."

Bud hadn't played for several years, but in a moment of weakness agreed to pitch for them on Saturday.

The powerhouse gang was to play the sawmill gang, and when the time arrived Bud's team took the field first. He strode to the pitcher's box, and sent down what was meant to be a fast ball. It went wildly wide, however, as did the next three, and the batter had a free walk to first base.

Bud feverishly rubbed dirt on his hands, took another stance, pitched four more times, and walked the second batter. He heard a man on the benches say, "He's just warming up. Watch what he does now." But what they saw was a repeat performance. As the third man walked to first base Bud hung his head in shame, and retired to the benches to become a spectator.

He found his failure was just what was needed to make these men accept him, however. None of *them* could get the ball across the plate, either. And none of them had been successful in the game of life. Somewhere along the way they had failed, many of them repeatedly. To see Bud as a failure like themselves made them warm toward him, and accept him as one of themselves. But they could not have been more mistaken. If anyone would prove through life his ability to swim against the current, like his native salmon, it was Bud Fisher.

Chapter 2

A PIONEER HERITAGE

In the mid and even late nineteenth century the east central area of the vast province of Ontario was known to the colonial powers, and political leaders in Canada's few cities, as the "Backwoods." This was well named, for it consisted of huge stretches of virgin forest, the home of various Indian tribes, as well as bear, deer, foxes, mink, and many other small animals.

Primary interest in that part of the country was as a source of furs for the European market, but soon the value of its timber was realized. Eventually most masts for British naval vessels were axed there.

On the banks of the York River, which winds through the forests, and along the lakes of part of that area, various lumber camps and small settlements were established, one of which later was named Bancroft.

Ontario stretches from the Great Lakes in the south across more than 700,000 square miles to the Arctic Ocean. According to geologists, when mile-high glaciers crept down as far as the Great Lakes in the ice age, they swept all the top soil before them. When they retreated this was left as rich agricultural land to the south, while in the north they left exposed vast stretches of granite rock, interspersed with innumerable lakes. Gradually huge forests grew on the thin soil remaining.

When an immigration policy was developed in 1853, many people from the British Isles and Germany left to start a new life in Ontario. They were given 100-acre sections of forest to reduce to farmland; in return they were required to maintain the road leading in. Unfortunately many found that after the backbreaking effort of felling trees by axe, the soil was too poor for profitable farming.

Others who came with a trade were more fortunate. One of these was Frederick Fisher, a shoemaker from LowHam, Somerset, who soon found his way to the new settlement at Bancroft.

There he eventually married Annie Maxwell, one of a family

of 15 children. Her father, James Maxwell, was born in Scotland, near the border. He later went to Ireland, and from there sailed to Canada. He lived in southern Ontario at first, but later took his family by ox-cart to the Bancroft area in 1867. He gradually cleared his land and a small community known as the Maxwell Settlement developed a few miles from Bancroft.

Seven of his 15 children were sons and most became farmers, too. Tom, however, started a harness and hardware business in Bancroft. Fred Fisher at first farmed and did what shoe-making he could near his father-in-law's property. It was here in a log cabin that his daughter and then Hubert were born. Then Tom invited Fred to work for him in the harness business. So the Fisher family moved to a big frame house on the village main street, with the York River flowing behind it.

Conditions were primitive, with no paved roads, electricity, plumbing or public transportation. Mail was back-packed in once a week. However it was a wholesome environment for a child to grow in. There was fishing and swimming in the river and nearby lakes in summer, and skating and tobogganing in winter when everything froze. Transportation was by horse and sleigh. Sometimes snow was piled six feet on either side of the main street.

Hubert was fortunate he was only a short walk from the school, and so did not have to miss much in winter. Children on surrounding farms often couldn't get out because of the deep snow.

Just before Hubert was ten, his younger brother caught some infectious disease, and the other children were quarantined from school. To help keep them entertained an aunt sent over some children's and adult books from a Christian publisher, since there was no bookstore in the village. Hubert's grandfather had become a Christian some years before when Plymouth Brethren evangelists had come to this remote area, and most of his children had also accepted Christ then.

With nothing better to do, Hubert read everything his aunt sent. He found he could understand even the adult books, and they set him thinking.

A few days later he awoke about 6 a.m. and couldn't get back to sleep. He kept seeing in his mind Christ carrying His cross to Calvary. It was a very sobering picture. He's going there to die for me, Hubert thought to himself.

After breakfast he went outside to get wood for the stove. As he was coming back, the awful realization that he did not know God really hit him. He dropped the armful of wood, and backed against the wall of the house saying, "Why was I ever born? I wish I had never been born if I'm going to be lost!"

This terrible despair lasted several moments; then the words of John 3:16 seemed to float into his mind. "God so loved the world, He gave His only Son, that whoever believes in Him should not perish, but have everlasting life."

Suddenly the truth of these words became crystal clear, and thankfully he exclaimed, "I believe, I believe!" Peace flooded his heart immediately, and he knew he was no longer lost but saved for eternity.

He then tried to live as he thought a Christian should. He attended the local Brethren assembly with his family, but he was afraid to confess Christ openly and was quite sure he would never make a preacher.

The summer he was 14 years old he went to work for an uncle who was a farmer 10 miles from Bancroft. A cousin six years younger still remembers how impressed they were when one night, in agony with a toothache, Hubert cycled all the way to Bancroft on that dirt road in the dark. Though the whole district is very hilly Bud cycled everywhere visiting his many relatives, an activity which later proved to have been excellent training for his future.

Every Bancroft boy climbed the Eagles' Nest "mountain," a craggy escarpment rising steeply from beside the York River a mile or so outside Bancroft. Indians once worshipped on this towering height, as well as keeping a sharp lookout for approaching enemies. In summer a breathtaking panorama greets the eyes, of forest-clad hills stretching miles in every direction, with the gleaming river threading its way into the distant horizon.

Bud sensed its beauty and was thankful he could grow up in such a place. And yet—what lay beyond? He had read of other places called cities which also had their attractions, and he hoped he would see some of them, too.

A few months before his birth, March 3, 1901, a railway line had been extended north to Bancroft, while later a small private line built to serve a mining area was also extended east to the village. Thus Bancroft station became quite busy with a station agent and three assistants. The population of Bancroft soon reached 600.

Bud completed his education at the village school, which then included two years of "continuation" or high school; afterwards he obtained a job as one of the assistant agents. Though the railways were originally built to serve the mines, the greatest revenue soon came from moving the many forest products south. An attempt was made to encourage passenger traffic, however, with the following advertisement: "The best fishing and hunting in Canada are found along this line of railway."

All station agents had to be telegraph operators. In addition to selling tickets, they were responsible for keeping a record of the engine and freight cars used to make up each train, billing and collecting charges for express items and freight, and, if time was short, they sometimes helped the tail-end crew with loading and unloading. The tail-end crew consisted of the conductor and two brakemen, who were responsible for signalling the engine, picking up the needed freight cars, and loading and unloading.

In his second year as assistant at Bancroft station part of Bud's duty was to act as agent on the small branch line going west. This involved travelling on it several days a week, leaving on the morning train and returning in the evening. One day the conductor came to chat with him for awhile.

"Bud, I hear your mother believes in being 'once saved, always saved.' Does she really?"

"Yes, and so do I!" responded Bud in surprise. That it was possible for a person once saved to be lost again seemed the most preposterous thing he had ever heard.

He at once determined to read the Bible for himself, to be able to prove to this conductor that he and his mother were right.

His father had recently given him a New Testament; so he now took this on the train, to read when he had time. It seemed a new book to him, and one morning he got so absorbed that he forgot where he was. A desk was provided at the end of the passenger coach for the agent to work on his records while travelling. Bud, suddenly realizing he should be working, quickly shifted his long legs from the desk top and asked the conductor if they were near Mumfords station. There was a laugh from the men then, for they had passed it three stations back, and Bud had work to do at each one.

He was conscience-stricken about his neglect; yet a seed had been sown in his mind, and he began to discover the importance of God's word and the riches it contained.

After Hubert was a trained telegraph operator, he was sent to various places on the C.N.R.'s network throughout Ontario. Once when he was in a very small community, he decided he would go to the nearest town, Capreol, on Saturday evening, in order to attend church Sunday morning.

A total stranger, he arrived at 9 p.m., and walked towards the YMCA intending to get a room for the night. Just across the street, however, he saw a church building. It was in darkness, but a room attached at the back had a light. He suddenly felt a strong urge to go in; so he tried the church's front door and found it unlocked. He felt his way to the back in the dark, until he saw a glimmer of light under a door. He knocked rather timidly, and a young man opened it.

Inside, Hubert saw eight people on their knees praying. So he knelt down, too; since no one else prayed, he eventually did himself. The others then all stood up.

"I guess you are the answer to our prayer," the young man said to him, smiling.

"What d'you mean?"

"Our pastor is on his honeymoon and has just wired that he can't get back for Sunday; so we came to pray for a speaker."

This was Hubert's first contact with a Baptist church, but he did his best. Later he met the pastor who thanked him for taking the service, and as an afterthought added, "Don't forget China, Bud. My wife and I are hoping to go there as missionaries."

That summer Bud was sent to another station further north, near the great Algonquin Provincial park, a wilderness with over 2,000 lakes and more than a thousand miles of waterway to canoe on. He was really looking forward to this and, hearing that the trout fishing was excellent in a large stream near the railway, he went there at the first opportunity. He propped his rod over a likely-looking place; then sat down to read while waiting for a bite.

It was a Christian magazine, sent from home, called "The King's Business," which he was reading. One article told how young men who had been truly converted went to some theological seminaries to train for the ministry and came out no longer believing in the inspiration of Scripture, nor the need for Christ's atonement for sin on the cross.

Hubert was so upset at this, he grabbed the fishing pole and found himself heading back to the station. As a youngster he had developed the habit of talking to himself and now, as he walked along the railway line he suddenly said, "What are you doing working for the railway? *You* know the truth, and you should be out proclaiming it."

He stopped dead in his tracks. Three possibilities flashed through his mind. "Shall I continue working on the railway in summer and go into the lumber camps preaching in winter? Or shall I quit the railway and preach full time? Or"—and the last possibility made his heart miss a beat—"shall I take the Gospel to the heathen?"

Immediately he seemed to visualize a multitude of oriental people, crowded together. He knew what that meant. God wanted him to be a foreign missionary.

That was the one thing he had always felt he couldn't and wouldn't do. But he didn't argue with God. Whether it was the effect of early home training, or the result of working as a telegraph operator who must obey instructions and deliver messages immediately, or just the result of his firm belief that God had spoken, once Bud got this message he was ready to obey at once. This response proved characteristic of the rest of his life.

Arriving back at the station he went straight to the telegraph keyboard and wired the chief dispatcher, saying he must go home at once. This was a very bold request, for there was such a shortage of telegraph operators that no one had been able to have a summer holiday. The reply came back: "An operator just discharged from hospital. Will send him right up."

As soon as the replacement arrived, Bud was on a train headed home. When he eventually reached Bancroft he went straight to the home of an uncle who was one of the three Brethren elders. Fortunately the other two were there visiting him.

"God has called me to be a missionary!" Bud blurted out at once. Then overcome with emotion, he sank into a chair.

The three men looked at him rather helplessly. Finally his uncle spoke.

"We've had no experience along this line at all. You'd better go to Toronto and talk it over with Mr. Irving."

It was a long journey to Toronto in those days, but Bud set off first thing in the morning, and fortunately found Mr. Irving, one of the Brethren leaders, at home.

They prayed together; then Mr. Irving gave his advice.

"You just keep praying about the matter, and the Lord will guide you."

17

Chapter 3

THE FLEDGLING TRIES HIS WINGS

Hubert accepted this advice, but had no inkling of how he might be led. Determined not to let any grass grow under his feet, he wrote at once to the railway headquarters. He asked for a six-month leave of absence, and a free pass for New York, since he imagined that was where he would sail from.

Right until a few days before his leave of absence was to begin, he had no idea where he was to go. His last assignment was to a station eight miles from Parry Sound, and he arranged to preach at the Presbyterian church in the morning and to a gang of railway men in the afternoon. However, the latter were called to duty earlier than expected, so he decided to go into Parry Sound for the rest of Sunday.

He was a stranger there, but happened to pass a Baptist church just as the evening service was starting. To his surprise he found the speaker was a missionary from China. He was more impressed with the fact that here was a missionary than with the message. After the service he eagerly approached the speaker with some questions. Later he went back to where the missionary was staying and talked until 10:30 p.m.

He then returned to the station, and asking the other operator for a piece of paper, was handed a cheap yellow sheet. On it he wrote the following to the China Inland Mission, dated Sept. 20, 1923.

> I feel called of God to be a missionary, and from what I have heard and read would like to go out under the C.I.M.
>
> I heard Bro. Meikle preach tonight, and had a talk with him after the service. He thinks I would be a suitable candidate, and advised me to write to you.
>
> I am 22 years old, single, and spent 2 years at high school. I was examined this spring, and told the physician I intended to be a missionary. He pronounced me in first class condition.
>
> I am a station agent on the C.N. Railway and have resigned. I shall be finished from Oct. 2nd. Would it be convenient for you if I come to Toronto then, and spend a day or two, if you

like. I am anxious to be off, and would go down to see you next Sunday, but I am holding services here.

Please reply early, and if you can, send me your application forms, etc., so that I can fill them out here, and save that much time. Mr. Meikle will be in Toronto soon, and will recommend me; also the Baptist preacher at Parry Sound.

Yours sincerely,
Hubert E. Fisher.

Finally Hubert got to bed well past midnight, his conscience clear that he had done what needed to be done. In his mind's eye he imagined he would be on his way to China by the end of October.

Poor Hubert! He had no idea of all that was involved in joining a mission, especially of the care with which the China Inland Mission selected its candidates.

He received a reply saying since he was coming to the city in a few days they would be glad to see him them. However no application papers were enclosed.

A few days later Hubert was sitting in the CIM office talking to their Canadian representative, Mr. E. Brownlee. The latter tried to convince Hubert, without success, that he should not plan to leave for China that week, but rather take the three-year course at Toronto Bible College!

Bud was non-plussed. He was sure God had called him to China, and he remembered that magazine article about young men who went to theological seminaries and lost their faith.

Fortunately just then Mr. Gibb, the Mission's Assistant Director in China, joined the discussion, and saw the disappointment and perplexity on Hubert's face. "How old are you?" he asked.

Hubert told him.

"That's too young. It would be hard for you to stand the climate. We find 25 is about the right age. Why not take a year at the Bible College first?"

That satisfied Hubert, and the fact that he registered at the Bible College and found lodgings that very afternoon, made a good impression at the Mission. As he studied, he soon learned there was much more about the Bible and missions he needed to know, and so he eventually completed the three-year course. When he got to China, and discovered that a fellow candidate, John Kuhn, had celebrated his 20th birthday in Language School, Bud finally realized how "canny" mission leaders need to be! However, John had already completed the course at Moody Bible Institute.

In the long summer vacations from Bible College Bud worked as a substitute agent for those on holiday. He thus earned money for his studies, and later outfit and passage for China. He also preached whenever he could.

Once he worked two weeks at a lake resort, and since the Baptist church had no pastor, Bud put up a notice in the station waiting room that he would hold a service there the following Sunday. At the bottom he added "No Collection."

When he arrived he was amazed to see the church packed out, and wondered if it was because there was no collection. An elder whispered that Lily Pons was there and would sing a solo. Bud had no idea who she was, but thought it was certainly nice singing. He therefore invited her to sing again after the sermon. The audience really seemed to appreciate it, so Bud preached another, shorter sermon, and asked her to sing once more. It was not until long after that Bud learned Lily Pons was a star of the Metropolitan Opera in New York.

At another place to which he was sent, as he approached the station building he noticed what he thought was the most beautiful woman he had ever seen. Her face "glowed like an angel."

He was delighted when the station master introduced her as his sister-in-law, saying she would be living in the private quarters at the back when his family was away, while Hubert would take care of the work in front.

Bud just couldn't get her out of his thoughts. He was strongly tempted to go in the back and try to establish a friendship, yet as a missionary candidate this was impossible. She probably wasn't even a Christian, and anyway the Mission rule was workers should be two years in China before getting married.

By the fifth day he was feeling he just couldn't resist any longer, when a package of magazines came in the post. Opening it he saw a copy of THE SUNDAY SCHOOL TIMES with the headline, "How to Get Victory Over Temptation." Eagerly Bud read the first point.

1. "Begin by admitting you can't do this in your own strength." At first Bud thought this crazy. If you gave up so easily, of course you'd fail, he reasoned. Then gradually he realized that all his efforts had been unsuccessful. So he accepted that point.

2. "See it as Sin." Bud felt indignant at this. It was perfectly natural, wasn't it, to be attracted by a pretty girl? He had no evil intentions. Yet he knew deep in his heart it wasn't God's will for him to marry this girl—therefore it would be sin for him to go against that revealed will.

3. "Yield the thing you desire totally to God." The most beautiful girl he had ever seen? And who had attended one of his meetings already? Yes.

4. "Trust for immediate deliverance." In a way, this seemed the most difficult of all. Hadn't he been struggling for five days, with no success whatever? Bud stared at it a long time, then took a deep breath. He poured out his heart in confession and trust, and never felt that temptation again. Even though the girl continued to attend his meetings, and accepted Christ, he was able to counsel her without any desire for a personal relationship.

The steps proposed in that article helped Hubert often. When he arrived at the already mentioned prison camp a little later, and went into the poolroom the first night, he was embarrassed to find some fellows still playing. He knelt down by his camp cot to pray, half expecting a boot to be hurled in his direction, and was astonished when the men at all three tables stopped playing, waiting for him to finish. He didn't pray very long that night!

No sooner was he in bed than he remembered Art's warning about poolrooms, and his mind suddenly filled with evil, sensuous thoughts. He tried desperately to dismiss them, without success. Then he remembered his previous experience, and prayed:

"Lord, I'm unable to stop these evil thoughts. I know they're bad and come from the devil. I refuse and resist these thoughts. I believe you will deliver me from them right now, in Jesus' name, Amen."

With that, he turned over, and fell asleep. This victory, and his acceptance by the prisoners through the fish and baseball experiences, enabled him to preach to them with conviction when the opportunity came.

He also found that as he took an open stand for Christ it gave courage to others who had drifted with the tide. At one station he had to share a room with another operator. In the evening the other employees were gambling, so Hubert went upstairs and lay on his bed reading his Bible. When his roommate came up and saw him his eyes brightened.

"Are you a Christian?" he asked. "So am I!" Then his face fell. "But I didn't have the courage to take a stand, so I've been gambling with the rest."

Another time three men were sitting in the waiting room talking, one a policeman, and one a businessman smoking a big cigar. Hubert by now cycled around selling Bibles and a few Christian books when he wasn't on duty, so seeing these men he asked if anyone would like a Bible.

"No," the policeman answered bluntly, "someone gave me a New Testament when I was in the army. I tried to read that last part, Revelations or something—I thought it the most ridiculous thing I've ever read. I never want to see it again."

They turned away, but later the man with the cigar motioned Bud into his office and showed him a big Schofield Bible. Shame-faced, he told him he was a Christian, and had been in the choir of a Toronto church. But when he had come here, with no Christian fellowship, he had gone the way of the rest.

"Now you are here, I want to take a stand," he finished.

"Good," Hubert encouraged him, "I'm preaching in the Anglican church on Sunday. You come and sing a solo."

The man immediately telephoned Toronto for some music, and when Hubert was unexpectedly moved away before Sunday, he asked this man to speak at the service as well as sing.

At another place a co-worker who was a nominal Roman Catholic heard Bud preach, and since he had no assurance of salvation, was very anxious to talk to him. The next time they were on duty together, he began asking questions, and Bud was so keen to help him he lost all track of time.

Suddenly the sound of a train whistle sent him leaping to the phone. There was no refrigeration then, and the incoming train was loaded with fresh fruit on its way west. These had maximum priority, and were only supposed to be in that station 20 minutes for a new engine, fresh supplies of ice and other servicing. Hubert should have wakened the engine and back-end crews two hours ago to have everything ready.

Now he begged them to hurry. Then he slipped into the baggage room and prayed desperately, "Lord please get me out of this big trouble."

Meanwhile the wheel tapper went about his job of knocking every wheel on the train with a hammer to make sure it was in good condition. In a few moments he appeared in the office, and asked Hubert to phone his supervisor to say a wheel was cracked, and must be replaced. Never did Bud relay a message with greater delight! The other gangs just completed their jobs as the wheel was replaced.

Did the Lord break that wheel to help him out of trouble? No, Bud decided. God knew the wheel was cracked and wanted him to have an undisturbed time talking to that young man.

While making God's plan of salvation as clear as he could in his preaching, Bud up to this time made no appeal at the end, since he was in each place such a short time, and there was no one to do follow-up. He felt the Spirit would bring conviction in His own time.

In addition to selling Bibles, Bud also carried a booklet called "The Traveller's Guide" and in one place a young man asked for 50 copies of this. A few days later a special Harvest Excursion train was to leave for the West from that station, and that morning this young man rushed in with another fellow.

"Bud, this man wants to accept Christ!" he exclaimed, and then dashed away while Hubert had the joy of bringing the other man into God's family. Soon he was back with two more, who also believed.

"Bring all who want to believe in together," Hubert urged, "there's no time to deal with them individually."

Before that train left, 25 men had sought Christ's forgiveness and cleansing in the station waiting room. And Hubert knew beyond a shadow of doubt God wanted him, like Peter, to forget his love of lake fishing, and become a fisher of men.

The CIM Council now had no doubt that he was a suitable candidate, and soon after he finished Bible college his passage was booked.

The day Hubert and the other candidates left Toronto station for the long journey to the west coast to board the ship for China, one of the CIM staff reported it thus:

"I shall never forget going down to the train to see them off. He (Hubert) didn't travel with the rest of the party, but hung about on the platform till the train was about to pull out. Then I knew why! On the end was a car crowded with men going to work in the harvest fields of the prairies, and he jumped into their coach, foregoing the roomier comfort of his own, in order to do personal work among them. An indefatigable soul-winner—that's what he is!"

Hubert, with characteristic humility, prefers the term "soul-seeker," but one thing he was sure of—that God had called him to be His fisher of men.

Chapter 4

A NEW WORLD OF DANGER AND DELAYS

Bud and the other men candidates from North America sailed from Vancouver on September 30, 1926. By October 25 they had joined others from Britain, Australia, and several European countries at the Mission's Language School for men at Anking.

He wrote his mother detailed accounts of life there, of which one must suffice here. In December he wrote: "You would laugh to see me studying in my room these days. I put on heavy underwear, then winter pajamas and shirt, then jacket and bathrobe, and heavy overcoat. And have a thick blanket around me!"

He also wrote about his fellow students, one extract being typical of him.

"I should be a kind of elder brother as I am the only one who has been a Christian more than about four years, and yet I am of them all the most critical and weak, and it is they who help me, not me them. Every day I praise God for brother Kuhn who is only 20, and yet I never met one who knew the Lord better, I think. I go to him for advice and teaching in the ways of the Lord."

His fellow students evidently didn't share his view of himself. John Kuhn often referred to him in letters to his fiancée, Isobel, who later wrote a chapter on him in her book, *Second-Mile People*.* John mentioned that Bud sometimes skipped meals if he began to feel spiritually dry with all the study, and would instead pray and pour over his Bible until his spirit was refreshed again.

When John sent Isobel a snapshot of himself and Bud she expected to see a very intense, serious face, and was amazed instead to find "a tall, slim, debonair youth, decidedly good-looking—with dimples!"

It was during one of these "pouring over the Bible until his

* published by O.M.F.

spirit was refreshed" periods that Hubert found what he termed his "life verses." They were part of Psalm 63 which speaks of thirsting for God, and the desire "to see Thy power and Thy glory . . . Because Thy lovingkindness is better than life, my lips shall praise Thee."

"That's what I'll go for, Your will, Your power and glory, Lord," Bud determined. He never forgot that purpose, and many times God was to allow him to see remarkable evidences of His power and glory in difficult and dangerous circumstances. Only twice did he lose for a brief time that joy in the Lord, and determination for His will which so characterized him.

He found language study fascinating, and was one of the few at the school to have continuous good health. At the end of the course in April his progress was recorded as "Very good indeed. Never afraid to use what he has."

The matter of greatest interest to most of the students was where the Mission would designate them to work. By now, however, Mao Tse-Tung's Red Army had begun to create danger in much of China, and strong anti-foreign feeling. The language students even had to hide for a day or two before they could escape by boat to Shanghai. By then several missionaries in the interior had been captured, and a few killed, so most were evacuated to Shanghai.

So crowded was the big CIM compound there that other houses had to be rented, including one for the men from the Language School. Here they continued their language study, and also spent time working with foreign troops stationed in Shanghai, a number of whom were won for Christ. Bud and John Kuhn were very active in this.

For a whole frustrating year, missionaries were confined in Shanghai, and while many found opportunities for service in that huge city, there was also much soul-searching as to previous methods of work, in view of the Communist accusations of imperialism. It was generally agreed much more effort was needed to develop Chinese leadership and make the church self-supporting. Once Bud grasped this concept he determined to go for it wholeheartedly, and it shaped his whole future ministry, as well as being a model to others.

While at Toronto Bible College he had heard a missionary speak about the very backward southwestern province of Kweichow, and he went and spoke with him afterwards.

"Why don't you come and join me, Bud?" the missionary had asked. "There's a tremendous need there."

Unfortunately this man and his little daughter were subsequently shot by bandits; now Bud felt all the more that Kweichow was where he should work.

One area of Kweichow had recently been allocated to Danish associates of the Mission, but as there was only one new Danish worker, "Yennie" Jensen, Bud was designated to work with him.

At last Chiang Kai Shek's armies repulsed the Reds and inland China was open again, but it proved to be another four months before Hubert and Yennie were able to reach Kweichow. They left by ship for Hong Kong, transshipped to Haiphong, then had three days in a train to Kunming, capital of Yunnan province. Here they were greeted with the unpleasant news that bandits were reported on every road, and the British Consul refused permission for anyone under his jurisdiction to travel further. They spent three months in Kunming, doing further language study and helping in the busy church life there. They were about to be assigned to work permanently in Yunnan when word came they could proceed to Kweichow.

They were 17 days on the road to Anshun, the city where they were to work for a few months with older missionaries, Mr. and Mrs. Pike, until they were more experienced to branch out on their own.

It was a rather discouraging church, and they didn't see one person accept Christ while they were there. Then word came that a single girl was being sent from Language School to the Pikes, and it was decided the two young men were now ready to be on their own in the area assigned to Danish workers.

They were to start in the city of Anlung, seven days south, which had a Mission house unoccupied for 15 years. There had been no rumours of bandits in the area for some time, but Hubert offered to go first and make enquiries along the way. If all was well, Mr. Pike and Yennie would follow with the baggage.

With a coolie carrying his bedding in a basket at one end of his carrying-pole and Gospel literature in the other, Bud set off. It was a mountain road most of the way, and they met few people, but no one had heard of bandits for several weeks.

They reached Anlung at last, and Hubert found an almost blind woman living in the gate-keeper's lodge. No one had touched the Mission house, since they believed it was haunted. So Bud sent the coolie back with word for the others to come at once.

It would take nearly three weeks for them to complete the journey so Bud had time to get settled, and pray fervently for his ministry in this needy area. He soon had a visit from the one Christian, a Mr. Meng, who had an interesting story to tell.

He had come to Kweiyang, the capital city of Kweichow, as a salt carrier from Szechuan province to the north, and finding nothing to carry back he had tried to get work in Kweiyang. Some missionaries needed a handyman; so they employed him.

"They didn't pressure me to be a Christian, but I was impressed with their lives and preaching. My problem was I was used to praying to idols, something tangible, and thought it must be very difficult to pray to an invisible god. Finally the idea came, why not go into the church and try?"

"And what happened?"

"I went in, and soon such joy and peace flooded my spirit, I took Christ as my Savior, and walked out born again."

Soon after this a missionary family was leaving to open work in Anlung, so Meng gladly went along to work for them. The wife became very sick, however, and they had to leave, but Meng decided to stay. There were quite a lot of Muslims in that city, and they tried to get him to join them.

"We accept the Old Testament as God's word," they'd say, "and Jesus just as you do, but we also have Mohammed who is the last and greatest prophet."

" 'But you don't accept Jesus as God's only Son, and our only Savior. That's where you fail,' I'd always answer."

Meng told Bud there was just one other Christian in the whole area, a Mr. Chang who lived 10 miles away in the country. When the missionaries left he gave his daughter to marry Meng, and they settled in the city, weaving and selling cloth. Word soon got around that Meng's yardstick was full length, unusual among the merchants, so business prospered.

"I longed for a chance to really prove to our Buddhist and Muslim neighbors that Jesus was the only true Savior, but when it came at last, it certainly wasn't in a way I would have chosen!"

"What happened?"

"A band of about 20 outlaws began to terrify these parts. They'd deserted from the provincial army with their guns, and fled to the mountains. From there they raided different towns and villages at night. The noise of shouting and shooting awakened us all one night, and most of the women and girls fled from home, trying to hide. Muslims prayed fervently to Allah, the Buddhists burned incense to their idols, but to no avail. I thought here was my opportunity to prove my God heard prayer, but to my horror, the robbers entered my house, too! Our baby was crying so my wife couldn't hide. It was awful! She pleaded for mercy, but they dragged both her and the baby off to join 200 other women they had taken.''

"But why just women?''

"They would later demand a ransom for them, and, if they didn't get it, would sell them as brides. There's always a shortage of marriageable women in China, you know. Girl babies are often destroyed, or in times of famine girls are given less food—so 200 women were worth a lot.''

"So what happened then?''

"In an agony I sank to my knees and prayed first that I'd get my wife back, and second that the baby wouldn't cry and annoy the bandits, otherwise they might kill it.

"But it seems the more I prayed in the city, the more the baby screamed up the mountainside where they were taken. My wife tried everything to stop it, but nothing worked. Finally in exasperation the robber guarding them gave her a push and yelled, 'Take that brat and get out of here!'

"My wife says she never moved so fast in her life! She ran, often stumbling, down that mountain path in the dark. The city gate had been left open by the robbers, so she was able to get right home. You can imagine how I thanked the Lord when I saw her. But do you know,'' Meng's voice changed to a somber key, "she was the only one of all those women to return! I've often thought that God didn't answer my prayer that the bandits wouldn't enter the house, in order to do an even greater miracle.''

God had turned his terrible minus into a glorious plus, Hubert thought. With such a man as Meng there to help them, the Lord would surely bring a harvest, he believed.

One of the first places Hubert visited was naturally the post office, where he was greeted warmly by the postmaster.

"As soon as you get a church building my wife and I will attend services,'' he promised.

Encouraged, Hubert reported this to Mr. Meng.

"That's because my father-in-law cast a demon out of his wife," he explained.

Hubert was then increasingly eager to meet Mr. Chang who soon came to visit the new missionary, and needed little encouragement to tell how he became a Christian.

A missionary had come to the city 20 years before, preaching and selling books in the market place. Mr. Chang, who was there on business, had never seen a white man before, so he stood and stared at this strange creature.What queer eyes, blue like a blind person's he thought, and what a huge nose! But the strangest thing seemed that Chang could understand his words.

"You all have a soul, and when you die, that soul will leave the body and stand before God to be judged," he heard. Could that really be true?

Soon the foreigner stopped talking and started selling books at only two coppers. That was a bargain he couldn't pass up!

As soon as he got home Chang began reading his treasure, a Gospel of Luke. He was very impressed by the genealogy of someone called Jesus, and thought from that he must be a very important man. He believed that in China only the descendants of Confucius kept such a table; one such descendant lived near him, and he was the 85th generation.

As he continued to read, however, the most practical part of the book seemed to him to be the story of the good Samaritan. It told how foreigners treated wounds: they used oil and wine!

A man living near him was having treatment for a wound, so Chang hurried over. He found a big black poultice had been prescribed, and this was actually keeping out the air, and keeping in the infection.

Chang excitedly told him how foreigners treated wounds, and carefully washed it with strong white wine, then poured on some oil. Very soon the wound began to heal, and that seemed clear proof to Mr. Chang that the Gospel of Luke was truly the word of God.

Further on he read how demons were exorcised. In his own village there was a demon-possessed man living alone, shunned by everyone. Mr. Chang decided he would try what he had read on him.

He set off, and found the man completely naked. Chang sat down beside him, prayed, and then faced the man.

"Unclean spirit, I command you in the name of Jesus to come out of this man."

The man then called out in surprise, "Where am I? Why am I naked?"

Chang explained what had happened, assuring him he was now free of the demon through the power of Christ, the Son of the true God.

News of that spread far and wide. Later, with the missionary, he cast demons out of twenty other people, including the postmaster's wife.

Hubert marvelled at this story, which certainly showed the power and glory of God, and also that Chang and his son-in-law had remained true to their faith all these years without any other fellowship. Yet he couldn't help wishing they had been encouraged to preach and teach, and lead others to accept Christ. He determined that in the future he would make it his business, with God's help, to turn Chinese Christians into skillful fishers of men, also.

Chapter 5

DOGGED BY A HOUND OF HEAVEN

Soon Mr. Pike arrived with Yennie Jensen, and stayed for a week, making sure everything necessary for taking up residence in a new place had been cared for.

"I think I shall take a different road back," he announced. "It will be a good opportunity to preach and sell Gospels in a new area."

"Do you know if that way is clear of bandits?" Hubert asked, with Meng's story fresh in his mind.

"I've made inquiries, and have permission to travel there. Things seem fairly quiet, as far as any place can be in these parts."

"What shall we do if we get word you've been captured by robbers?" Hubert persisted.

"Do nothing," Mr. Pike replied firmly. "If we once yield to a ransom demand, then no missionary will ever be safe travelling."

Hubert and Yennie were relieved to receive a postcard from him, written the second night, saying, "Crossed Saddle Mountain with a party of soldiers. Thankful for that protection."

The next day their relief was shattered when the two coolies who had accompanied Mr. Pike appeared, weary and empty-handed.

"We spent the third night on Green Mountain, and next morning brigands captured Mr. Pike, and ordered us to come back and see what ransom you'll offer," they said.

Full of concern, Hubert sent them to Mrs. Pike with the news, telling her he would go at once to see what he could do to free her husband.

Then he went to the city hall for permission to travel to Green Mountain. The magistrate flatly refused it.

"We hear now there are bandits on every road," he said. "If you go they will seize you, too. Leave it to us. We'll do what we can to free Mr. Pike."

They waited for 10 anxious days without news, then Hubert

felt convinced that he must go. He went to the magistrate again, saying no matter how serious the danger, he must leave in the morning.

The magistrate once more urged him not to, but seeing Hubert's determination he finally admitted some soldiers were leaving for that direction in the morning. "Go with them, if you must," he concluded.

Hubert hired a carrier for his bedding, and the two of them swung in behind the soldiers when they marched off. When they finally reached Green Mountain village Hubert was very thankful to find Mr. Crofts, a veteran missionary from north of the province, had been there for three days.

"I've discovered robbers use this village as a hide-out, and useful look-out point," he told Hubert. "The men wearing turbans are bandits."

As Hubert looked around it seemed to him the majority were wearing turbans! One evening, too, their innkeeper's sons were openly counting their spoil, unconcerned at anyone seeing them through the open door.

One of the first things Hubert noticed was that every house in that village had a fierce-looking dog in front of the door, and at the approach of a stranger they growled and snapped until the owner came to see who it was. He was therefore amazed that when he walked down the main street, the dog from the inn would follow him, about six feet behind. When Hubert stopped, he stopped. Once when they were passing a large house set back from the road, five fierce dogs rushed out at them. The dog from the inn ignored them until they were within a few feet, then shook his head once at them. Immediately they hung their heads and slunk back to their house.

Upon returning to the inn the dog resumed his position at the door, and completely ignored Hubert, and he the dog. Yet each time he went out the dog followed.

It took nearly a week before they got details of Mr. Pike's fate. A band of fourteen brigands had carried him off. When he refused to bargain with them they stripped him to his underwear, tied him to a stake, and left him outside through the cold night. When he still refused to negotiate a ransom they shot him and threw his body in an underground river.

Since there was nothing they could do now for their friend, with aching hearts the missionaries prepared to leave. But wouldn't the village bandits be preparing to rob them after they left? It was a frightening prospect, and they prayed earnestly for God's protection.

The answer seemed to come in the form of a troop of soldiers who appeared from the opposite direction and spent the night in the village. They willingly consented to the missionaries joining them, and they all left at daybreak.

All went well, and they were thinking how fortunate they were with this protection when about noon they reached a part of the mountain road which looked an ideal place for robbers. Suddenly the captain spurred his horse and galloped off, his soldiers running behind him as hard as they could. In a moment the missionaries and their carrier found themselves alone.

"What do we do now?" asked the terrified coolie.

Mr. Crofts thought a moment. "Well, we're about half way to the next stage. We might just as well go forward, don't you think?"

Hubert agreed, and glanced a little fearfully behind. Then he exclaimed in astonishment, "Look! There's the inn dog following us!" Hubert then shouted at him, and threw stones around him to frighten him off, but still he stuck with them.

After not meeting one person or passing a single dwelling all day, they reached an inn about 8 p.m.

"Look at this fine dog," Hubert said to the innkeeper. "He's been following us since daylight, and has had nothing to eat. If you'd like to have him, give him some supper, tie him up in the morning, and he's your dog."

The astonished man said he would certainly keep the dog.

It rained that night, and when they set out next morning the road was covered with ice. They had a hard time keeping their feet going down the mountain, but at least consoled themselves they had got rid of the dog. They had been slithering along an hour, when in an effort to hold his balance Hubert found himself looking back up the mountain.

"Just look at that!" he cried, pointing.

About a hundred yards behind them was not only the original dog, but also the one from the inn where they had slept the previous night. The men shouted, glared at them, and threw lumps of ice towards them, but to no avail. The dogs kept coming, but always stayed just out of reach.

No one else seemed to be travelling that bitterly cold day, until about noon they saw one man coming towards them.

"Do you think he's a robber?" asked Hubert.

"It's hard to tell from here. We'll just have to keep going."
As the man drew near he smiled. "My, you are lucky!" he said.

What a joker he must be, Hubert thought to himself, and couldn't help asking, "Why do you think we are lucky?"

"Look at those dogs following you! In these parts we believe that if a dog follows a person it's a sign he's being protected by the spirits. No one would dare to touch you with a dog following you, and here you have *two* dogs with you!"

They didn't throw any more ice or stones at the dogs after that! But neither did they feed them, for they could be in serious trouble if anyone thought they were trying to steal the dogs.

For four days those dogs followed them. Then they met up with some soldiers.

"Where are you going?" asked Mr. Crofts.

"Anshun."

That was where Crofts needed to go to break the sad news to Mrs. Pike. But Hubert, of course, was returning to Anlung.

"I think we'd better keep together in the circumstances," the senior missionary decided, and Hubert agreed with unexpected warmth.

As soon as they had joined the soldiers, Hubert looked back to find the dogs had disappeared, their mission evidently accomplished. How strange were the workings of God!

As they passed through the gates of Anshun Hubert was conscious of a quickened heart beat, even though they were bearing such tragic news. God had sent those dogs to protect them, he had no doubt, and brought him back to Anshun so unexpectedly. What further blessing did He have for him here?

Chapter 6

BUD FINDS A THOROUGHBRED, AND BECOMES A PIONEER

On the ship from Shanghai Hubert had written to his mother: "No doubt you would feel happier to know that I was either engaged or married to a suitable girl, but I am praising the Lord that he has kept me free, and now that I am off to the interior I will have no choice in the matter for a couple of years I expect."

Indeed, in Language School he had earned the label of "confirmed bachelor." Evidently some others thought a wife would be "a good thing" for him, and did their best during the long wait in Kunming. He tells his mother he had offered to babysit one evening for a British family, and adds, "Fearing I would be lonely they had sent along Miss Sands from the hospital, too. She is one of the finest girls I have had the misfortune (sic) to meet. What she said to me about the Gospel makes me wish I could hear her deal with a soul. Seems to me she could persuade anyone to accept Christ if persuasion would do it. She is very gifted and well educated . . .

"Yesterday Brinks and his wife invited Yennie and me to go for a walk with them to see a mountain temple. Miss Sands and Miss Tyndal came along, and we had a very pleasant time. I had been praying earnestly for those two girls as I know how zealous they are . . . and how little encouragement they have. So I had private talks with both, and God gave me exceptional liberty in pointing out to them that we 'are complete in Him.' "

No doubt his mother hopefuly tried to read between the lines, and prayed in faith. More than three months later, October 27, 1929, just a few days after Mr. Pike's capture Hubert had written to tell of that, and continued with something which may have given his mother fresh hope.

"I am enclosing a picture taken just before I left Anshun for here. You will recognize all but Miss Binnie. She is a new recruit, and from appearances is a good one and will doubtless be used much by the Lord. Her coming to Anshun was a cause for thanksgiving in many ways. I was told repeatedly in

Shanghai that I should not waste my golden opportunity of getting a wife there. In Kunming I said to myself that the two young ladies there were at least as fine as those I met in Shanghai. And last of all comes this young lady. I am not at all interested in her, but I declared to myself about the second day she was there that she sure is a thoroughbred, and appeals to me more than any other I have met in China. I only say this to illustrate the verse 'Who works for them that wait for Him.' Nevertheless, I tell you I didn't waste much time in Anshun after she arrived, or I'm afraid my bachelor ideals would soon have been on the rubbish heap.''

Now here he was back in Anshun through no planning of his own. He was sure now: it was God's will that he should marry Mary Binnie. As usual, Hubert was ready to obey directly when he heard the Lord's command, but out of respect for Mrs. Pike's sorrow, he thought he should wait a few days.

In spite of her grief, Mrs. Pike realized how much the men had been through in their efforts to trace her husband, and prepared a real feast for them, with duck, and other delicacies.

On coming into the living room afterwards, and finding Miss Binnie alone, sitting on the couch, Hubert decided now was the time. He immediately went up, put his hand on her shoulder, and told her he loved her and would like to marry her.

In utter astonishment she exclaimed, "But this is so sudden!" Her response was no storybook answer to gain time. Mary had heard in Shanghai that there was a "confirmed bachelor" in Kweichow, and hadn't given him another thought. In fact she had never dated in her life, since at a young age she was drawn to the mission field, and none of her contemporaries were interested in that.

Hubert told her God was leading him to start new work in an area where Christ was completely unknown. He planned to live in primitive inns and try to be as much like the people as possible in order to break down cultural barriers, and make the love of Christ visible by his life as well as by preaching. It wouldn't be easy, but he was sure that was how the Lord was leading. Would she be willing to join him in this kind of life?

If Hubert had told her something of what he had shared with mother about his feelings for her, instead of just talking about the work, perhaps he would have had more success. Mary admired what he was attempting, and felt sorry for his having to live such a lonely life, but knew she could never marry a person out of pity.

She said she must think about it, and prayed much the next two days, and also consulted Mrs. Pike who thought it would be too hard a life for a young wife. Mary believed Hubert had just asked her because she was the only one around, and so her answer in the end was "No." But she tried to soften it by telling him if she ever felt differently she would let him know.

Hubert took comfort in that, feeling sure the marriage was God's will, and it would come about in His good time.

He returned to Anlung and immediately entered whole-heartedly into the work he had described to Mary. He and Yennie were the only missionaries in five whole counties so he had early decided he would go and pioneer another county, leaving Yennie and Meng to build up the work in Anlung.

A travelling colporteur, Mr. Huang, happened to come to their area just then, selling Bibles and books, and Hubert saw this as a God-given help in starting. So he, Huang, and a new Christian named Wang set off on a two-day journey to a place called New City. About 4 p.m. the second day they were feeling very weary from walking on cobbled streets since daybreak but hurried on for fear the city gates might close. Since no one had clocks or watches one was never very certain at what time they would be shut. In spite of their prayers, they were too late, and had to sleep in one of the horse inns outside the city, where robbery was more frequent.

After breakfast of rice, red peppers and pickled beans, three elderly women came in. Hearing a foreigner was there they expected him to have medicines, and wanted him to see a sick friend nearby.

Hubert told them he had no medicine, but if the sick person would have the idols removed from her room they would come and pray for her.

They soon returned, disgusted that the family had refused to move the idols, and thus were missing a good opportunity for healing.

The women were invited to sit down, and Mr. Huang explained the Gospel while Hubert went into an adjoining room to pray for them.

An hour later Huang called Hubert to come and see three new Christians! He was surprised the women had believed so readily, but when he saw their radiant faces he couldn't doubt it. It was only later that he learned how one of them, Mrs. Lee, had actually been prepared, 30 years before, to respond to the Gospel.

She had been coming in from the country leading a donkey loaded with rice, when three robbers sprang out and tried to snatch the rope. She resisted, and one man stabbed her with a dagger, leaving her unconscious by the roadside. Lying thus, she saw a man in white approach her with a look of compassion. He bent down, touched the wound and said, "You will be all right now."

She regained consciousness, and was able to walk into the city, and for 30 years wondered who that man was. As soon as she heard the Gospel she identified him as Jesus.

After the women left, the three men went to the market, put up some posters and a hymn sheet and started to sing, thus drawing a crowd. They each preached 10 to 15 minutes, stopping between sermons to sell books.

One man who bought a Gospel said his name was Hoe, and that he lived in a place called Corn Patch. Hubert smiled as he made a note of it. The man had only a thin cotton gown on, but listened a long time, shivering in the cold.

On Sunday Huang and Wang went off to evangelize in the country, leaving Hubert to hold the first Christian service in New City. Mrs. Lee and four other elderly ladies met with him in the inn kitchen, and all sat on short stools on a mud floor around a mud stove.

Again he told them the Gospel story, and they listened intently. When he spoke of the resurrection of Christ, and told them of the future resurrection of each Christian's body, Mrs. Lee stood up and excitedly pushed Mrs. Duan's shoulder.

"Did you hear that?"

"Yes, I did. Because Jesus has risen from the dead, and gone back to heaven, we can go there, too!" All the ladies then jumped up and danced around the room for joy.

"We must celebrate this!" declared Mrs. Duan, and soon had a pot of green tea ready which they drank to the Lord.

They were too excited to listen any more, so Hubert closed this unorthodox Sunday service with a short prayer. Inwardly he, too, felt like dancing for joy over this demonstration of the Lord's power so early. All the months he had been at Anshun no one had become a Christian. Now he knew why God hadn't answered their prayers that they get inside the city to sleep!

Once more He had turned their minus into a plus.

At the end of a week Huang moved on, and Hubert and Wang returned to Anlung. On the way Wang pointed towards a hill and said, "That's Corn Patch where Mr. Hoe lives."

"Oh! Let's go and see him then," said Hubert, for they had been praying for him every day.

"This is a lonely, robber-infested road. We shouldn't stop," warned Wang. They went on a few yards, then Hubert stopped, convinced they should go and see him.

As they went up the hill Hoe's was the only house visible, but there were remains of several others which had been burned down.

Hubert imagined Mrs. Hoe would never have seen a white man, so he waited around the corner while Wang went to the door.

Soon Hoe came out and greeted him warmly. He was now a happy believer! He told Hubert he had been working down the hill a few days before and suddenly saw the grass on fire, with the wind blowing towards his bamboo hut. He prayed frantically to all the gods he knew but still the fire advanced, and finally caught the corner of the roof. Then he remembered the Gospel he had read, and cried out to that God. The wind changed and blew out the fire on his roof, but all the other houses were burned. That had really convinced him of the Gospel's truth.

With these encouragements Hubert returned to New City as often as possible, and others believed. This led to various forms of opposition, and even rock throwing at some open-air meetings.

Once Hubert had the help of two travelling evangelists for a few days, and when they both left for another city they met a man who confided to them he was an opium addict and gambler. His luck had been so bad lately, he was sure it must be due for a change, and he was now going to a certain city to gamble.

"Don't do that," they advised, "go to New City instead, and find the foreigner there. He will tell you how to be delivered from opium, and how you can get eternal life."

That evening, after Hubert had finished preaching from the inn doorway, this man, a Mr. Wang, told them he had been an opium addict for 14 years, and measured on his little finger the large amount he needed a day.

"Is it possible," he asked wistfully, "that such a person as I could be delivered, and get eternal life?"

"Certainly it's possible. Stop smoking at once, and come over in the morning as soon as the craving comes on," Hubert assured him.

He expected him about 9 a.m., but at 5 o'clock he was awakened by pounding on the inn door. Since no one answered it, Hubert finally went down himself. There stood Wang.

"I'm craving my opium now!" he blurted out.

Hubert took him to his room and sat him down.

"You'll be delivered all right," he said with a confidence few others might have felt, "but there are some things I must explain first. One, I want you to understand salvation is God's free gift to us. You can't earn it, you don't deserve it, you simply accept it as God's gift to you."

"That just suits me," Wang said. "If you had asked me for anything, I couldn't have done it. Once," he continued, "I went to a temple for two weeks trying to break off, and gave them a lot of money, but I left worse than ever. I've taken all kinds of treatments, and nothing works. But I can take a gift."

"Second, you know, Mr. Wang, that you have sinned against God in smoking opium, and in other ways too?"

Wang knew he had sinned against his parents by smoking opium, but that it was against God was a new idea to him. After Hubert explained further he finally agreed.

"Third point. If you trust in Christ as your Saviour, and stop your evil ways, people will laugh at you. Are you willing for that?"

"Let them laugh!" he answered vehemently.

"Finally, will you now take Jesus Christ, the one God sent to save us, as your Saviour?"

"I will," Wang said firmly.

"When you receive Christ as your Saviour, God accepts you as His child. God is now your Father. Let us pray to Him, and ask Him to take away your craving for opium."

"I can't pray. I've never done it."

So Hubert told him to repeat some sentences after him. Soon Wang stopped him.

"I feel all right now," he said in a surprised voice.

Hubert talked to him a bit more, telling him to close his opium den, and read the Gospel he said his son had bought. And, if the craving became strong, he could come over again.

At 5 p.m. he was back, beads of perspiration on his forehead.

41

"I've got through the day reading and praying, but now I can't stand it any longer. I *must* have a little opium —just a little," he pleaded desperately.

"No, no," Hubert said, "we'll pray together again."

Wang could pray himself this time, and after they had both prayed he said, "I feel all right now."

For ten days he came morning and evening to pray with Hubert, and as they prayed the craving would leave him. On the tenth day he told Hubert he would be gone for two weeks, selling the straw sandals his wife made.

"Don't go," Hubert urged. "You know everyone will be smoking opium in the inns, and you'll go back to it."

"No, I have a Protector now. When I reach out my hand in prayer, God reaches down and grasps my hand and holds me," Wang answered simply.

When he came back two weeks later, the craving had gone for good. At first no one believed it when he told them, they knew him too well. Some thought Hubert paid him to say he was cured. When they saw he really was, they thought Hubert had used powerful magic, or special medicine. They soon bought out his stock of Epsom salts, quinine, and worm medicine, but no one was cured from opium addiction through those.

At last many believed it was as Wang said, through faith in Christ as his Saviour. Over the next months at least a dozen more were cured. But in the midst of all this demanding and exhausting work, Hubert did not forget his "thoroughbred."

Chapter 7

A PASSIONATE DESIRE

One day in New City market, a thief stole Hubert's glasses from his pocket. Unable to read without them, he had to make the 10-day journey to Kunming.

The doctor at the Anglican Hospital gave him a prescription, but Hubert was dismayed to find he could only get the lenses in Hong Kong, entailing a month's wait. That afternoon he happened to visit a missionary who kept several pairs of glasses for any one in need. One pair felt good, so Hubert took them to the doctor and found to his joy they were exactly what had been prescribed.

The military was suddenly very busy in the area, however, and commandeered every horse and coolie available, and no one else was able to leave the capital. An unusually large group of missionaries were thus marooned there, including John and Isobel Kuhn.

Isobel writes of the joy with which John told her that Bud Fisher was there, and that Bud had invited him to spend the night in prayer with him.

John returned a chastened man in the morning. He told his wife that after prayer, Bud had said there was something he must say to him. He had been disappointed hearing John preach the night before, feeling he showed pride in his mastery of Chinese, rather than a yearning to reach the lost. And John admitted this was true.

It is interesting that while everyone had recognized that Fisher would make a good missionary and was an excellent personal worker, one or two in their assessment of the new recruit thought he might not be leadership material, and might be easily swayed by others. This thinking may have been a result of his quick response to the call to missions and China. Throughout his missionary career he showed no desire to be concerned with administration and directing the lives of others. He was always happiest seeking out the lost and strengthening the churches. Yet when he saw a spiritual need, he had no hesitation in taking the lead.

Now, thrown in the midst of this unusually large group of missionaries, mostly strangers to him, he was quick to recognize something was wrong. In fact there was deep disunity, and a splitting into factions which was hindering growth in the churches.

So Hubert, one of the youngest there, when asked to speak at the weekly prayer meeting, proposed a time of special waiting upon God for personal renewal, and revival in the churches. The provincial Superintendent and his wife heartily agreed, and Isobel Kuhn was one of the first to break down in confession of wrong attitudes.

All but essential work was stopped, and the missionaries gave themselves to prayer. After 10 days a real and lasting work of the Holy Spirit had changed the hearts of all. The travel situation then suddenly eased, and all were able to return to their work, cleansed and refreshed. Thus, through Hubert, God had changed a frustrating delay into another plus.

Back in Anlung he longed to see something similar in his own province where the churches were even weaker than in Yunnan. He had made no attempt to keep in touch with Miss Binnie, but wrote to Mrs. Pike and others on the need to pray for revival.

Mary Binnie, writing to her parents on March 15, 1931, told of sin in the Anshun church, and of much opposition faced there. She continued:

"A number of us are feeling very strongly the need for revival in the hearts of us foreigners before the Lord can work among the Chinese," and adds that she and her co-workers had begun to set aside an hour at noon for this, and found they could still get just as much done the rest of the day.

"I think I told you before that Mr. Fisher, a young Canadian in the southwest of our province, who was the means the Lord used last year to bring revival to the foreigners in Yunnan, is much exercised about our own province, and has been spending hours a day in prayer . . . He has become so burdened that I think he'll go mad if there isn't a break soon."

She then quotes nearly three pages from a recent letter Hubert had written Mrs. Pike, in which we find the following:

"In the midst of these barren, so heart-breaking years, make known that Thou art the God who answers by fire, that Thou *dost* hear the cry of the humble, that Thou *wilt* turn the desert into a beautiful garden. Last year at Anshun all of us together did not wrest one soul from the jaws of Satan . . . How passionately I desire that our Superintendent call a conference of missionaries before Mr. Hsieh [a Chinese evangelist] comes to the province. Or that we foreigners covenant to pray daily for at least two hours for renewal in the province *this year*. Why am I so anxious a conference be called? First, that things not right among ourselves may be put right; second that we may pray seven or eight hours together daily. Thus we might recover a lost art—that of carrying a burden of prayer till the anguish becomes so intense it gives birth, or at least puts us in the attitude where we can pray 'the prayer of faith.' . . . How feeble is our praying! I feel sure the sparsity of results is due to our feebleness in prayer.''

It seems a little unusual to quote three pages from someone else's letter. One suspects Mary wanted to give her parents some understanding of this Mr. Fisher. It was only a short time after she wrote that home, that Hubert received the letter she had promised if she ever felt differently about him.

She had had time to see that his desire to ''go native'' was no passing fad, but a deep conviction of how best to promote the Gospel of Christ, and it was getting results. Then his passionate desire for revival struck an answering chord in her. So while Hubert was seeking with his whole heart to please God, God was preparing to reward him with the treasure he had realized would be a worthy fellow labourer.

He joyfully read the letter, and would have rushed off to Anshun to become engaged in person, but unfortunately Mrs. Pike was then in Shanghai. It would be bad in Chinese eyes for a man to visit two unchaperoned young ladies. All they could do was plan by letter for the wedding in about 10 months, and hope they could meet soon.

When a Mission leader in Shanghai heard of the engagement he remarked Fisher had indeed ''fished out a good one.'' In fact Hubert believed Mary had been designated to Kweichow purposely, as a suitable wife for him. Certainly she proved ''a good one.''

Born in Scotland, Mary had emigrated to Canada with her parents when she was eight, and they settled in British Columbia. Her mother had been a Salvation Army officer, and they were still associated with the Army, though Mary accepted Christ in a Methodist Sunday school when she was 12. She had always had thoughts of missionary work, having a grandmother who prayed one of her children or grandchildren would become one, but it wasn't until she was 17 that Mary fully yielded her life to Christ.

After two years of university she attended Teachers College, and then taught in a remote area of B.C. While there she heard of the great need for women doctors in China and contacted the CIM. When lack of finances prevented her from going to medical school, she trained as a nurse.

While everyone spoke in highest terms of Hubert's Christian character and gift for personal work, a few were more guarded concerning sound judgement and common sense. No doubt his giving up his job and asking for a ticket to New York, when he didn't know where and with whom he would go, might appear immature or lacking in common sense; however with a Brethren background it wasn't so strange to go without formal training.

As John Kuhn said to his wife, "Bud isn't like other people. He views things from a different angle." Instead of "common" sense he seemed to have an unusually acute "divine" sense, a heavenly perspective, of what God desired, and acted without delay or argument. When he later received his share of his father's estate, common sense might have regarded it as a useful provision for the future needs of a faith missionary. Hubert, however, thought of Christ's words to "sell all you have and give to the poor," a practice he has continued through life, even selling some of their few oriental keepsakes (after retirement) to help finance a new building for a mission to Vancouver's skid row.

In Mary God provided Hubert with all he needed to complement his own gifts. Her judgment and common sense were rated in superlatives by those who knew her, and equally highly her Christian character, ability to lead people to Christ, and gift for teaching. And she was now ready to share all the deprivations Hubert deemed necessary, as well as his desire for revival. Whereas Hubert once thought of marriage as a minus for the ideal missionary, with Mary it was to prove a real plus, for together, with her gift for teaching, they accomplished far more than would have been possible alone.

Some weeks after their engagement, Hubert received a telegram which sent his spirits soaring. "ESCORTING SUTHERLAND TO CHUNGKING. COME IMMEDIATELY. MARY."

He was busy until 2 a.m. preparing for his unexpected absence; then he packed, and was up for an early breakfast. Unconsciously he was whistling so loudly it brought a visiting missionary down to ask, "What's all the racket about?" Hubert's blushing explanation, "to keep up my courage," didn't fool the visitor.

It transpired that another Kweichow missionary, Mrs. Sutherland, was ill, and Mary, as the only available nurse, must accompany her to the nearest hospital, in Chungking, 15 days from her station. Since Chungking also had a British Consul and Hubert and Mary as Canadians could then only be legally married at a consulate, the Superintendent had decided it would save two long journeys if Hubert went now to be married.

He wrote of his first day of travel in a letter to his mother from Chungking, 12 days before their wedding.

"Had a good day and kept going until nearly dark. I recall the first time I travelled that road I was fagged out after I did half the distance, but this time was fresh as a daisy. Trust and expect that Mary will always be such an inspiration and spur to me that I can do twice as much as before she was mine, and always be refreshed by thoughts of her. Have been in the same house with her now for 9 days, and so write confidently.

"The trip to Anshun is 7 stages. I would have made it in 3 or 4 I expect, but was delayed by my carrier who was not in love, so it took 5 days.

"Arriving in Anshun I found the butterfly had flown,and there were no foreigners there. I stayed over Sunday, and preached in the morning on 'The Love of Christ constraineth us.' I had been so conscious of the constraining power of love."

From there he was able to travel on the new, unpaved "motor road" to Kweiyang, where he found Mrs. Pike and Ruth Campbell, Mary's co-workers, there with others for the Bosshardt wedding. Mary had already left with the Sutherlands.

Hubert stayed over for the wedding, telling his mother how surprised the Chinese were to see a happy-looking bride,—(their brides often don't know their husbands, and are supposed to weep at leaving home.) He added, "Everyone here in Chungking knows we have come to get married, for Mary's face is just radiant, and I guess I look happy, too."

In spite of his hurry to see his bride, the day after the Bosshardt wedding Hubert had persuaded the gathered missionaries to stay on for a day of prayer for revival, before scattering to their various destinations. He then made up for lost time, doing the remaining 15 stages on truck, foot and riverboats in 11 days. As he neared Chungking the strange circumstances might well have made him nervous. He had met Mary only twice, for a few days, the last time being nearly 18 months before, when she had turned him down. Hubert didn't worry about that, however. He was certain this was the girl God had chosen for him, and that was enough.

Chapter 8

A DIFFERENT SORT OF HONEYMOON

For the sensitive Mary, the prospect of meeting this man who was almost a stranger, yet with whom she would be on such intimate terms in three weeks' time, did produce a little apprehension, in spite of the certainty that it was God's will. She needn't have worried, however, for both had experienced so much on their long journey that there were many things to talk about. In fact, it was only through God's miraculous intervention that Mary was still alive. Mr. Sutherland described their journey in his prayer letter.

"The trip ordinarily takes 15 days, but we took extra coolies to get to Chungking in nine days if possible. So there were four men to carry my wife's stretcher, and two extras to change with them; three men to carry Miss Binnie's chair and two extras, . . .

"On the seventh morning we engaged two boats to take us down river, thus avoiding the road through the worst mountains and hills . . . It had rained the night before, and there were many waterfalls along the banks, some hundreds of feet high. The narrow gorges were beyond description,—I've never seen so much natural beauty in a short space. There were many turbulent rapids. The skill of the boatmen in shooting these will always be a wonder to me. You think you are heading for certain destruction when the boatman turns the rudder and sends the boat shooting at tremendous speed past the rocks you expected to crash into.

"After about three hours of shooting down the most scenic river I ever travelled on, we came to the Dragon Rapids, the worst on the river. The water rushed with a deafening roar through a narrow channel between two walls of rock, falling in three steps of six or seven feet each to the next level, where it whirls and eddies till it comes to the next rapid 200 feet farther on.

"Coming down river, the boat stops just above the Dragon Rapids, and passengers must get out, walk over a rough mountain path, then scramble down through rough boulders below the Rapid, to get into the boat again.

"Meanwhile the boat is let down the rapid from the rock wall, the boatmen all standing and holding tightly on the ropes attached to the boat. While three or four men hold their ropes firm, others take new positions. Then they all slacken together, and let the rushing water carry the boat a few feet further. Then the first group take up new positions, and so on, until the boat is lowered bit by bit through the rapid.

"They insisted my wife's stretcher could not be taken over the mountain path, and therefore she must remain in the boat as it was lowered through the rapid, while Miss Binnie and I walked over the path. We refused to leave my wife alone in the boat, however, so they began to lower it with the three of us in, while the boatmen held the ropes up on the rock.

"When they got it about halfway down the rapids, the current became too strong, and swept the boat with such force that the men had to let go of the ropes or be carried into the water themselves. There we were racing along, far from the rock wall, the ropes dragging after us through the water!

"I shouted to Miss Binnie that the ropes were gone, and we both grabbed bamboo gaffs and tried to pole the boat away from the worst part of the rapid. It was useless, however, as the water was too deep for the gaffs.

"Before we could do anything else, the boat struck a rock near the bank, throwing the prow of the boat up against a rock on the shore. The boat stuck on top of the rock, and I rushed up to the prow, and jumped out to try to hold the boat from slipping back into the rushing water. A boatman scrambled down at the same time, seized a rope and caught a loop on a rock further up the bank. This prevented the boat from being carried away, but it and the stretcher were tipped at a 45 degree angle into the water.

"More boatmen arrived now, and sent me and Miss Binnie up the rocks. They then pulled my wife off the stretcher, and carried her with much difficulty to the prow where others took her and carried her up the bank. What a relief it was to see her out of the boat and on solid rock! It certainly was God's deliverance. He made the craft stick on just the right rock . . . He kept the stretcher from tipping into the current . . . .

"The men held the boat on the rock until the stretcher bed and baggage had been carried ashore. Most of the boxes had to be pulled out of the water which flooded the boat. When they had done all they could, they pushed the boat off, and it disappeared under the rushing current . . .

"So there we were with our soaked baggage scattered on the rocks around us . . . Finally we engaged another boat, and the owners of our second boat, which was still above the rapids, were persuaded to lower it to the place where we were waiting. The sedan chair and other things had to be carried over the rocks, and put back after the boat was lowered through the rapids.

"Finally we got away after two hours. We only had a few more rapids after that; then the river became smooth. We landed before dark; then had the job of drying all the wet clothing over a charcoal brazier and hanging it on lines stretched across our room in the inn. Miss Binnie and I didn't get much sleep that night . . . ."

In fact Mary hadn't much sleep most of the way, for her patient required much nursing care. Fortunately they had to wait three weeks after registering their intention to marry; this gave Mary time to get rested after the patient reached hospital, and to get acquainted with Hubert before the wedding.

On the morning of July 11th, they went together to the British Consulate for the legal ceremony. They stood in front of the consul's desk, and he asked Hubert, "Will you have this woman to be your wife?" On hearing Hubert's "I will," he asked for Mary's, then said, "I pronounce you man and wife," and handed them the certificate.

"Is that all?" asked the astonished Mary, "I don't feel married!"

This came later, as she told her family.

"The Consular wedding over, we were whisked off in two sedan chairs across the Yangtse river up into the hills to the CIM summer home for the ceremony which to us was the one that counted . . . It didn't matter that I was married in a borrowed wedding dress and veil, or that even the wedding ring was borrowed. In that beautiful setting in the flower-covered hills, with lovely wild flowers for my bouquet, and in the presence of eight guests, Mr. Sutherland pronounced us man and wife."

They had Sunday up there, Monday they packed, and Tuesday set out on the long journey back. As they travelled, Mary rode a sedan chair while Hubert walked. The first 10 days they had to sleep at Chinese inns. On the first night they had just settled down and Hubert was almost asleep, when he heard an exclamation from Mary.

"Something's bitten me!"

"Take no notice. Just turn round and go to sleep."

But the practical Mary got out her flashlight and soon found a bedbug. According to Hubert they spent the next two hours killing 48 bedbugs. Mary worded it this way to her family:

"The first night on the road we had an *awful* time with bedbugs which utterly ignored our oil sheet (spread beneath their bedding.) We literally killed hundreds on our sheets and mosquito netting, and then when we arrived back Hubert and I wore blisters on our fingers trying to wash out the blood stains. That night we decided to graduate from Chinese beds, afterwards sleeping either on doors or boards resting on two benches. We searched the bedding each night for any lingering guests, and think they were all exterminated by Tsunyi, 10 days later . . .

"The journey was a happy one. We were up before 4 a.m. each day, and I walked a few *li* (1/3 mile) with Hubert; then when I got in my chair I would read to him our Scripture portions for the day as he walked alongside . . . ."

They were glad to get to Tsunyi, even though they found the Robinsons and other workers had gone up to a mountain temple to give tracts to thousands of pilgrims attending a ten-day festival. They had left word that they hoped the Fishers would join them.

It had been much on Hubert's mind that perhaps on their return to Tsunyi the Lord might lead them to call all missionaries of the province to come there to pray for revival. So it was disappointing to find the Robinsons, who were also looking for revival, were to be away so long.

After praying about it they did go up the mountain, and there sensed that Mr. Robinson was really expecting Hubert to go ahead and arrange something, since he had been the one God had used in arousing others to the need, both in Kweichow and Yunnan. Meanwhile everyone begged them to stay up there at least two days.

It was from here that Mary had written her letter about the wedding, and continued:

"Well, you will not be surprised to hear that we are very very happy together. Coming up here has been a trial to us in a way, for we have practically no time alone. Here at this temple we are never out of sight of the Chinese . . . But I think we'll appreciate each other's company more than ever, if that's possible, when we can be together again. Mrs. R., Miss Stair and I sleep in an improvised upstairs, with oil sheets and curtains for walls, and climb up a ladder to get here, while Mr. R., little Sandy and Hubert sleep below.'' That would not be most people's idea of a honeymoon, especially as a thief broke in one night, and took Hubert's razor, soap, and umbrella.

With Mr. Robinson's encouragement they wired the Superintendent for permission to invite all missionaries there for a prayer conference beginning August 12. The reply said, ''Proceed if you consider proposed meetings sufficiently important.''

Hubert felt the burden of responsibility for the meetings then, and spent much time in private prayer, while the others wrote the invitations.

He also held meetings with the Chinese, and during the conference the man who was causing the most trouble in the local church truly repented and confessed his sins. A German missionary at a neighbouring town who was near death with typhus, was wonderfully healed as they prayed at the conference. Altogether they felt great things had been accomplished in many hearts, and looked in faith for results in the churches.

The Fishers reached Mary's former home August 25, and while she went through station accounts for the last six months with Mrs. Pike, and finished packing, Hubert went off to a tribal area where the work was much more encouraging than that with the Chinese.

It was September 5 before Mary had time to write home to report on the August prayer conference, saying: ''We have been, and still are very rushed.''

She had kept a carefully-written diary while single, but wouldn't let Hubert read this. Overcome with curiosity one day he peeped at the entry for July 11, to find the one word, ''Married.'' It was rather ego-shattering, and he ruefully reminded himself that temptations yielded to usually turn out disappointing. Of course, Mary, having had no time or privacy, had had to fill in essentials later.

To her parents she expressed her feelings more freely. Writing while busy with the accounts, she told of Hubert being away in tribal country for a prayer conference. ''Then three days ago the rest of us went up. It was *so* good to see my dear boy again, and we had a very happy time together that evening. But alas, it wasn't to last.'' The district military general sent up an SOS in the morning for Mr. Chen to go and treat his eyes. Mr. Chen was the other main speaker with Hubert, and since he was being much used there, it was decided Mary would go back and treat the general.

Six weeks after the wedding they were back at Hubert's "home" in an inn. Soon Mary wrote, "I have been alone here five days, and it seems like five years. I don't think I ever knew before what it meant to be lonesome. Hubert has the same feeling, and if he had only his wishes to consider, would have returned immediately. But he was on the King's business . . . ."

So as they joyfully looked forward to serving the King together, one in heart and purpose, Mary early experienced that this would often involve being in separate places.

There was just one thing she did express her personal preference about; this was that, apart from his old friends, her husband should now be known as Hubert rather than Bud.

Chapter 9

THE BREAKDOWN

Hubert had now been in China five years, and after the physical drain of a month's walking, much of it over mountains, to his wedding, and the heavy spiritual burden of prayer for revival in his province, plus constant meetings and pioneering efforts, he began to feel really in need of a holiday. Having recently spent so much time away to get married, however, and with a real breakthrough in his own area, plus a number seeking help to overcome the opium habit, he told himself this was no time to slacken his efforts.

Mary gives a graphic picture of what he was accomplishing at that time:

"There has been much blessing in the Hingi district lately—a number of definite conversions, and a real *seeking* after God—and it is largely due to the activity of the new Christians that the Gospel is being spread. Hubert's aim is to get them from the start to realize it is a *Chinese* church, not foreign, and they are responsible . . . Like Paul, when he gets a work started he leaves it to the local people and goes elsewhere, returning from time to time to encourage and admonish them.

"Our idea is to live as simply as possible. In this we are departing from what has usually been done. That is, we want to be reckoned on a level with the average Chinese instead of being looked up to as a higher class. In this way we expect to reach all kinds, and make them feel we are one with them. Hubert and Mr. Jensen have been doing this with results far exceeding those in other parts of the province, but of course, what single men can do cannot always be done by a couple. Some of the younger workers are looking to see how we get along, and if we are successful, will follow."

Mary was ready to do all she could to meet Hubert's ideals, and she tells of walking up to ten miles now, in cloth Chinese shoes, since foreign ones were no good on cobble stones and rough mountain sides.

She concludes, "Opportunities for preaching the Gospel are

more than we can take advantage of . . . our own wisdom is utterly insufficient in knowing how to carry on the work.''

Once again she is alone and tells her family, ''I constantly find myself wishing he (Hubert) might arrive today. But the work needs him at Sincheng, so I must be content, and the meeting will be all the sweeter. He says I wear well, and the longer we are together, the more he appreciates me, and I feel the same. We are very happy.''

She also mentions that the foreign-style house in Anlung seems ''a real hindrance, just as it was in Anshun, for it gives the idea of wealth, although nothing wonderful from our point of view,'' and adds that she doesn't have a servant, ''which shows we are only common people, too.''

For the next year letters are full of preaching opportunities, opium addicts cured, several demons cast out, and various medical cases Mary cared for. They believed world conditions pointed to the near return of Christ, and Mary wrote, ''We feel the time for witnessing is short, so we want to give ourselves to the work just as much as is consistent with maintaining good health.''

Fifty years later, it seems they were perhaps guided more by what many other Christians were saying and writing at that time, than from divine insight. With the best of motives, Hubert had worked himself to the point of a breakdown. Some of the damage had been done before marriage, with the eating of often indigestible foods, and too much red pepper, plus the lack of holidays, and all Mary's care could not undo this.

Eighteen months after their marriage, in a letter thanking her parents for the second wedding ring which had arrived safely buried in a fruit cake (the first never got there) we find this ominous paragraph.

''Hubert has been a little better since it was decided we remain here. [Annan, another more distant area Hubert had opened when others came to join Jensen.] Privately I feel sure only furlough will make him fit again. If he speaks for four or five minutes his head gets very bad. So he hasn't taken any meetings since returning to Annan.

''I feed him Ovomaltine, (I bought a tin when we were married, and it has come in useful now) and eggnogs with plenty of powdered milk in them. We don't use a lot of milk as eggs are so cheap here, but now I'm not stinting on anything.''

Hubert improved a little after that, but by the following

spring had deteriorated so much that they were asked to go to Shanghai for a medical examination and probable furlough.

They had a very hard, dangerous overland trip, followed by rough seas from Haiphong, and they both arrived in Shanghai a month later in poor physical condition. They were recommended for furlough at once, Hubert with the rather ambiguous diagnosis of "brain fag." Actually he couldn't talk to anyone, read, or even think without feeling pain between his forehead and left ear, and his blood circulation was badly upset, as well as his stomach.

He had expected that after two or three months' rest he would be back to normal, but after spending months at Bancroft his head was still as bad, though he took some meetings. The friends and relatives there were very glad to see him, and although they were beginning to experience the Great Depression economically, they joined together to give Hubert the money for a new suit. A few were not altogether pleased to hear later that someone had passed a used suit on to him which fit, and so he had given the money to a person he thought in greater need.

They later moved to Mary's relatives in Vancouver, but still there was no change in Hubert's condition. At last, when they had been home two years, the Mission's North American Director wrote saying they should give up the thought of returning to China, and find work at home.

It was very painful news, for their hearts were still in Kweichow. But after reading that letter a verse came into Hubert's mind: "I have set before you an open door which no man can shut." A great peace came over him then, for he felt it was God speaking to him.

At no time did Hubert ever feel that God had treated him unfairly after all his devoted service. Nor was he rebellious, but always believed that God had a purpose and would somehow bring good out of it. He also had a strange conviction that the time lost through this illness would be made up to him at the end of his life.

Meanwhile, where could he find a job in his condition, and at the depth now of the Great Depression? His thoughts naturally turned to the railway, and he finally got a temporary job as time keeper at Prince George, B.C., which meant being separated from Mary.

He found no difficulty doing that work, and after a few

months he was offered the job of relieving station agent, which he had done before going to China. He was told it would start in November, two months later, and that he would be the first permanent man to be hired in three years!

Just a few days after receiving this promise of permanent work, a letter came from Mary to tell him Mr. Canfield, the CIM Representative in Los Angeles, had written saying if they hoped to return to China he should leave the railway at once, and do two months deputation work with the Mission, then see how he felt. Mr. Gibb, the General Director, would be on the West Coast then, and would come to Vancouver to interview him.

What should Hubert do now? Unemployment was so high. Should he risk giving up this promised job and live by faith for two months, meeting many people in speaking engagements which usually caused a recurrence of his headaches?

He dropped on his knees to pray in his bare little rented room, and immediately that familiar, overwhelming sense of peace crept over him. He understood it to mean he should leave the railway.

The following day, however, he received another letter from Mary. This was in reply to his last to her in which he had mentioned his head being bad. She wrote: "I guess we better give up the thought of going back to China since your head still bothers you so much."

Again Hubert knelt down, and this was his prayer. "Lord, I must apologize for bringing this matter up again since you gave me such clear guidance yesterday, but you see this letter I have just received from Mary."

Immediately he felt again that wonderful sense of peace. He resigned from the railway, and returned to Vancouver.

They did the two-month deputation trip arranged by the Mission, and at the end Hubert felt no worse, perhaps a tiny bit better.

"Those with such a bad breakdown as yours are never sent back to China, for they soon break down again," Mr. Gibb began in the interview. "However, first Mr. Canfield, and then Dr. Glover felt convinced you should have another chance, since you both did such valuable work there. Do you think you can stand it?"

"Yes, if we go back to Kweichow," Hubert answered eagerly.

"That's the last place I would send you. That's where you

broke down, and the people there would expect you to keep up your old pace," Mr. Gibb answered with finality. "I shall send you to the other end of the country for a real change. You will be much closer to medical help there, too."

Chapter 10

DEATHBLOW TO DESPAIR

Alone again, Hubert and Mary stared at each other, shock written in their eyes. They had agonized so often in prayer for the people of Kweichow, and seen God do wonders in that difficult area. Surely this was a mistake!

"I just can't believe it," Mary said at last. "And the dialect will probably be quite different somewhere else."

"Yes," Hubert's voice was hoarse with stress. "Don't they realize how our hearts are with those Kweichow people?"

"Of course—that's just it—and there's always so much needing to be done," Mary was beginning to realize that medically there was sense to this idea. But would Hubert?

He paced up and down, his head throbbing. Then he remembered that verse, "I have set before you an open door which *no man* can shut." He stopped and squared his shoulders.

"I believe they are wrong," he said slowly, "but God can overrule their mistakes. He can turn this horrible minus into a plus somehow. We'll trust Him and go."

"The other end of the country" meant northeast China and they found themselves designated to a large, highly organized work, with many problems, about 60 miles south of Peking, in Hopei province. Hubert felt miserable inside a conventional, high-walled mission compound like some feudal lord, shut away from the common people. Within three months he had deteriorated so much he felt he couldn't last more than another month in China. He would have to write a letter of resignation to the Mission.

As this thought was filling his mind he heard a Sunday school class singing:

"Trusting in the Lord your God
Onward go, onward go . . . ."

Through it God seemed to assure him He would strengthen him, and they would not have to go home. A few days later they were asked to take charge of a Mission rest home for two months, in Shansi, the province to the west, and they went with relief.

While at the rest home, the Japanese, who had recently invaded China's east coast, advanced to Peking, and it was impossible for the Fishers to return. So after their stint at the rest home, they were asked to wait at the city of Linfen, where the CIM had a hospital, until a new designation could be given them in Shansi.

By now, Hubert's peace of mind had drained away; he again felt they would have to return to Canada, and he really lost his joy in the Lord for the first time since being called to be a missionary. It was a four-hour train trip to Linfen, a famous old Chinese city with a six-foot bronze head of Buddha. But Hubert had no interest in sight-seeing, and nothing Mary said seemed able to cheer him up.

"I feel stifled with these great eight-foot walls around me," he exclaimed one evening. "I've got to get outside."

He strode past the gate-house of the hospital compound with an energy born of desperation. He felt he had to be alone with the Lord. Yet once outside, the intensified pounding in his head slowed him to a dejected stroll, as a feeling of utter depression overwhelmed him. He and Mary would have to leave, that seemed certain. Yet how could they all have been mistaken? And why didn't healing come?

He thought back to the various remarkable healings in Kweichow. He remembered Wang, the opium addict who had been cured in 10 days, then many others. Hubert could see them all now as he paced outside the compound wall with increasing frustration. How was it they were healed in days, yet nothing had really eased his head in three years?

He knew no amount of pain, frustration or trial should rob him of his joy in the Lord, however, and it was this horrible sense of loss which had driven him out into the shelter of darkness for some desperate prayer. He shivered, suddenly conscious he was in shirt-sleeves, and it was almost 10 p.m. In five minutes the hospital gates would be locked for the night.

At that moment Mr. Wang's response in face of *his* desperate need came back to him: "I can receive a gift."

"Why," Hubert chided himself, "here you've been praying for hours and getting nowhere. Don't you remember it's by *believing* we get things from God?''

Hastily and fervently he prayed, not for healing, but for that which he missed so much.

"Lord, I believe that you restore your joy to me *now*." He raced back as the gate was closing.

Sleep came almost instantly as he lay down, and in the morning he found himself full of a joy which never left him again. Mary was greatly relieved, but still there was the question of where they were to go, and if Hubert could stand it physically.

In a few days the letter came. "It's from the Super," she said.

"You read it. Where are they sending us?"

"A place called Yicheng. There is no missionary or pastor there at present, but a Pastor David Yang has had to evacuate from the east and is coming soon. There's a boys' and girls' school in the compound, but they're closed temporarily," she hesitated a moment, "because of the threatened Japanese advance. Do you think you'd be able to stand that happening?"

"Time will tell. I suppose it's another of these big compound places. How utterly wrong they are! Are there opportunities for pioneering?"

"I should think so. We can do what we like if we are the only ones there. And there are two single girls a couple of hours away. I expect they will be glad of help."

"We'll go then, and trust the Lord to undertake," Hubert declared with a touch of his old enthusiasm.

Mary uttered a silent prayer of thanksgiving. All their household things were at their first station, but she had been used to simple housekeeping in Kweichow. She'd manage somehow. All that mattered was that Hubert was ready to go. But suppose the Japanese did come? How would he be then?

Chapter 11

THE JAPANESE ARE COMING!

Slowly Hubert's health began to improve in Yicheng. With a pastor and very capable Bible woman, Miss Lu, to care for things in the city, he began visiting the many villages around by bicycle, since the nearby terrain was much flatter than in Kweichow. Meanwhile the Japanese had continued their westward advance.

On the morning of March 1, a letter arrived, and Hubert opened it.

"It's from the Super," he told Mary. "He says that since the Japanese are getting so near, we should invite as many women and girls who wish, to shelter in our compound until the Japanese advance has passed us. As we are foreigners, they should be safe from the unwelcome attentions of the soldiers."

"Do you mean just the Christian women?"

"No, they're doing such horrible things; I think we should give an open invitation in the city to any who want to come. Then we can tell them of Christ, too!"

"It's a good thing this compound is so big, after all! But how can we feed so many? It's hard to get vegetables for ourselves now. So many are afraid to be out in the fields."

"Oh, they'll bring their own," Hubert said optimistically. "We'll tell them to. You ask Miss Lu and the pastor to get word to the Christians, and I'll go to the magistrate."

They both hurried away, and in a short time the majority of Christian women in the city and surrounding villages, as well as quite a few others, arrived with bedding and a supply of wheat and vegetables. Before next nightfall 80-90 women and as many children tried to make themselves comfortable in the day school buildings, and various other rooms on the compound. There were also a few men, either church leaders, or some obviously disabled who were allowed in. Many more men wanted to come, but this would have aroused the suspicions of the Japanese.

As city after city in the east fell before the Japanese, most major universities evacuated ahead of the advancing armies,

63

intending to start again in the free west. Some students walked a thousand miles to catch up with their colleges, while others whose homes were in the still free area in the east waited there until they knew where classes were to resume. In Yicheng there were four such students from the same medical college, and they thought it would be useful, and even entertaining, to learn English from the foreigners who were now here.

Hubert agreed, on the condition that they use an English Gospel of John as the textbook.

"It seems a pity to get tied up with such a small group, when so many villages are begging us to go," Mary had protested, "and students are often too proud to listen to the Gospel."

Hubert agreed with her as day after day he explained a passage, and urged them to accept Christ. They would merely smile, their interest being only in hearing English.

On the afternoon of March 4, only one student arrived in Hubert's study as he sat with rather gloomy thoughts about how the Japanese were hindering the spread of the Gospel. Back and forth went the uninspiring conversation in rather stilted English, and inwardly Hubert felt impatient as the visitor stayed on past the end of the hour.

His eyes wandered to a magazine on his desk, and a paragraph headed with the large Chinese character for NOTICE. He hadn't learned it in Language School, or later, so he idly began to practice it with his finger on the desk. It consisted of 11 strokes, each of which must be in the correct shape and size. He doodled this perhaps 50 times, having no idea how much he would need that character the next day.

Suddenly they were interrupted by the sound of running feet, and a knock. Hastily Hubert opened the door, and there stood a breathless messenger from the magistrate.

"The Japanese are only an hour away. Get out as fast as you can," he panted, then sped away.

The student jumped up in alarm, exclaiming, "What shall I do? What shall I do?"

Most people would probably have said, "Get going!" their heads filled with thoughts of their own safety. But not Hubert.

"The first thing to do at any time is to get right with God. Why don't you just now get on your knees and receive Christ as your Saviour?" he suggested.

The student immediately knelt down and prayed. Then thanking Hubert, he quietly walked out the door.

"Well," Hubert said to himself as he watched his guest disappear, "that fellow would never have believed without the news of the Japanese coming, I'm sure. Perhaps their coming won't be all minus after all."

The fact that this student had become a true believer was confirmed two years later when Hubert and Mary met him in free China.

There was no sign of the Japanese that night, and March 5 dawned with no sound in the usually bustling, noisy city. After they prayed, Hubert and Mary made their rounds. They found 30 women huddled apprehensively in the large room of the girls' school while four or five men sat quietly in the gate-keeper's room inside the eight-foot high entrance which opened on the main street.

Suddenly from the direction of the city's north gate came a strange rumbling sound, then buildings began to shake on both sides of the main street as three tanks charged through. They were each manned with soldiers grasping machine guns and glaring intently at every building they passed; seeing no one, they ground on and out through the south gate, and back to their base.

In the ensuing quiet, a few Chinese men crept back into the city to rescue some of their abandoned possessions, but before they could leave again Japanese infantry poured in from every direction.

One man thus caught was a Mr. Chang. He was passing the door of the mission compound just as he saw the soldiers coming from north and south. So he pounded frantically on the massive gate, calling out his name.

He was known there, for his wife and teenage sons were earnest Christians, and he had often been prayed for, but would never go near the church. The men in the gate-keeper's room hastily unbarred the door, and let him in just in time. In utter relief he sank on the chair offered, and when he had regained his breath, wondered at the peace and confidence of the Christian leaders around him.

"This refuge was here just when you needed it," they pointed out when he was calm enough to listen. "All you did was call out, and we let you in. Heaven's gate will open for you in the same way. The only condition is that you must *want* to come in."

Mr. Chang's jaw dropped, and strong emotion gripped him

as he understood their meaning. He prayed, confessed his sins, and trusted in Christ, becoming the first convert that day. Hubert thought, "How often we've prayed for him, and his heart always seemed hard as stone. But how quickly the Japanese invasion has accomplished what all our efforts had not. Yes, this is not going to be a minus situation after all."

Then Hubert did a foolish thing. Above the sound of marching men and orders shouted in a strange tongue, could be heard anguished Chinese protests. Curious, he unbarred the huge gate, opened it a crack, and peered out.

Soldiers headed in both directions were passing by, while two Chinese, hands high in the air, were being searched and robbed. Hubert quickly tried to close the gate again, but the movement had been seen, and three heavily armed men pushed their way in.

Making the best of the situation, Hubert smiled warmly and invited the men over to his quarters. Mary had just set the breakfast on the table, and immediately the soldiers jabbed at the food with their bayonet tips until everything was eaten.

Hubert then politely tried to lead them back to the gate, but the men had other ideas. They opened the first door they came to, and found two young Bible women there. The soldiers gathered round Miss Lu, the more attractive-looking, and thrust their faces close to her's with a leer.

This will never do! I must find the Japanese general, Hubert thought, and get him to order his troops to keep out of our compound!

Fortunately Mary had watched where the soldiers went, and immediately came to help protect the girls. So Hubert rushed away, to find to his dismay that the gate was wide open, and soldiers were pouring in.

He dashed out and there, right in front of him was a high-ranking officer riding a horse in the midst of some foot troops.

Hubert broke through, and grabbed the officer's saddle, calling out in English, "I want a notice forbidding soldiers to enter our property!"

The startled commander stared in astonishment at a white man dressed in long Chinese gown, holding his horse and talking gibberish. Seeing he didn't understand, Hubert said it in Chinese, but still there was only a blank look. Turning to an aide, the officer motioned him to get an interpreter.

The man stepped out of rank, turned north, and was soon

back with another man.

"I want a notice forbidding soldiers coming on our property," Hubert repeated in Chinese and English. But the interpreter, either Korean, or from another dialect area, still didn't understand.

In desperation Hubert seized a stick and wrote in Chinese character on the mud street, "I want a notice . . . ." Chinese characters have the same basic meaning in Japanese though pronounced very differently, and the two men understood at once. How Hubert thanked God for causing him to practice that character the previous day!

The aide quickly took a piece of paper out of his bag, and wrote a sentence in Japanese, then handed it to Hubert.

Zig-zagging a hurried path through the crowd, Hubert raced back to the room where the three soldiers were. He waved the paper in front of them, and immediately they stood up, saluted, and marched out.

Next Hubert showed the paper to the soldiers nearest to the gate. "If I'd pointed a rattlesnake at them they couldn't have been more dismayed," he said later. "Each on seeing it paled, saluted and went right out. We tried hard to read it and the signature, but failed. I pasted it on a board, and its effectiveness never diminished."

That night they went to bed under the Japanese rising sun flag, full of thanksgiving for God's help and protection. Mary had been wondering very much about the effect of the day's events on Hubert. As he prayed, however, he appeared full of confidence in God's help through all the difficulties and dangers he could see ahead.

Chapter 12

INVASION DANGERS AND DELIVERANCES

In the morning, terror reigned outside the compound walls. Groups of soldiers filled with lust for women and loot were going from door to door. Some women, who had stayed in the city, either climbed over the wall trying to flee to the country, or fled to the mission refuge. Many with bound feet somehow scaled the 12-foot high compound walls, and in their terror seemed ready to jump down, until the women inside shouted they would bring a ladder.

Just as the Fishers finished breakfast they had their first official visitor. Somehow he had persuaded the men to open the gate. When Hubert and Mary looked out their window they saw a husky-looking officer, revolver at his belt, and pockets bulging with what Hubert guessed to be hand grenades, heading purposefully towards their quarters.

Fearful now, Hubert could do nothing but open their door with a rather unsteady hand, and nearly fell over at the officer's first words in rather halting English.

"I am a Christian. My father is a pastor in Japan."

The astonished Hubert showed him in, and he immediately began to empty his pockets, not of hand grenades, but canned foods of various kinds which he wished to give them.

He had seen the sign "Gospel Hall" on the gate, and those characters were used for the Christian church in Japan, too.

He was the General's secretary, and even more valuable to them than the food was this officer's name card which he left with them. With that in his hand Hubert knew he could go anywhere and feel safe. In fact, he was delivered from some evil-intentioned men on several occasions by showing that card. He felt from this encounter God was teaching him not to see trouble when there was none.

He was still talking to this officer when a woman ran up and shouted in Chinese, "The Jap soldiers are on our wall, and going to jump down!"

Hubert quietly told the woman to go back. Then he suggested

to the officer that since their conversation had been interrupted anyway, he might like to look around the compound. He led him first, of course, to where the soldiers were on the wall. The officer addressed them in Japanese, and without a word they hurriedly got down and disappeared.

That first Japanese army left that following day, and once they were gone all the remaining women in the city came pouring into the mission compound, bringing food and cooking utensils. Each had a tale of horror for the women within the compound. All had been raped and abused, except one old lady who knew a little Japanese. She had called out she had an infectious disease.

By the day's end there were 118 women, 20 men, scores of children, and four donkeys on the premises. During the next weeks six different Japanese armies went through the city on their way to the front lines at the Yellow River, staying from one to nine days. Each time they came they shelled the city before entering, and bombed surrounding areas. Once a cannon was set up only 200 yards from the compound, so the noise was frequently deafening. But as Hubert wrote philosophically, "We got used to it, and suffered no harm."

Indeed, his headaches had largely disappeared. The necessity of having to trust the Lord completely in many new situations, and having to think of the needs of so many others, had brought about final healing.

Meanwhile the Christians were not losing any opportunities of witnessing. Miss Lu soon held two evangelistic meetings a day, with help from the others in personal counselling. Mary had classes for children, at which they learned many Bible verses and choruses, and many seemed to truly trust Christ as Saviour. Hubert visited the villages whenever there was a period of quiet.

Most kept very healthy during this time, but one elderly woman, who came in with her husband, had a heart attack after being there a month. She was his second wife, and had lived in daily fear that the spirit of the first wife, dead several years, would harm her.

She had had a very sad life, but before she became ill the Christians had talked to her about Christ, and she accepted Him. As a result, fear of the former wife disappeared. Just two hours before her death three days after the heart attack, she said to the other women, "My sins are forgiven. I'm not afraid to die. I'm going to be with Jesus."

This made a deep impression on others who were not yet believers, for they knew her former life, and had never known anyone to die unafraid of demons.

The Japanese were not the only source of danger. As soon as the first invading army had left, a band calling itself the First Army of China entered the city. Actually they seemed to be a horde of brigands coming for loot. In face of this new danger Hubert thought it best to visit their leader, and obtain protection as soon as possible.

He found the man smoking opium, which wasn't a very favourable sign; but on learning who Hubert was he greeted him very cordially.

"I was educated at a Methodist Mission school," he said, "and I know you Christian people do a lot of good. My army was attacked by the Japanese east of here, with many casualties, so I have come hoping to get recruits to replace them. I'm afraid many join up just with the hope of getting plenty of plunder."

He readily gave Hubert an order forbidding his men to enter the mission premises.

Some of these had come from far up in the mountains, and had never seen a foreigner. On the way back from seeing the leader, one of the soldiers, thinking Hubert must be a Japanese, rushed at him with fixed bayonet. Fortunately the pastor who accompanied him jumped in front of him just in time, and explained who Hubert was.

Hubert's policy of "going to the top," wasn't always successful, however. In July a Japanese army came across the mountains directly east of Yicheng, and seemed full of ill-will towards the population, and missionaries in particular. The Fishers learned later this army had come from Yangcheng where they suspected missionary Gladys Aylward (of THE SMALL WOMAN fame) had secretly passed information of their movements to the Chinese forces. This had resulted in the Japanese being ambushed, with heavy losses.

The first morning, a Japanese officer with several soldiers pounded on the compound gate, demanding to see Mr. Fisher. He was very rude and arrogant.

"We are placing a guard at your gate. No one may go out or come in," he barked.

"We have 138 refugees here, beside animals," Hubert protested. "The well water is undrinkable. We have to go outside the city to get the spring water. Please give me six permits for men to go out with the water cart."

"You cannot use the cart. Here are four badges. Take them to the Commander's office this afternoon to get them stamped," he snapped. "Only four men may carry water."

"But we are right out of water *now*," Hubert pleaded. They took no notice, and marched away.

In the early afternoon Hubert went along to the Commander's office with the four badges, hoping he would be reasonable and grant the required six. The guards, however, refused to let him in; instead one of them took the badges to be stamped.

Soon he came back with the bad news that the Commander absolutely refused them permission to get water. Hubert alone could go.

In spite of repeated warnings not to speak back after an order had been given, Hubert was desperate, and continued to explain to the unfriendly guard that soon all would die of thirst, for he alone could not carry water for so many people and animals.

"Surely Japan would not treat innocent people who had not fled from them, or done them any harm, in such a way?"

"They are Japan's enemies, and ought to die," he answered gruffly.

To the guards' surprise, Hubert refused to leave. They all looked angrily at him, and menacingly handled their weapons either in exasperation or to intimidate him.

Soon a higher-ranking officer came along. Hubert buttonholed him, explained his predicament, and asked him to go with the messenger to see if the Commander would relent.

Very unwillingly, the officer finally went, apparently to no avail. The messenger was soon back, angrily declaring, "*No passes!*"

Hubert now felt he'd reached an impasse and had better get the Christians to pray. As he went he suddenly experienced a feeling of joy as he sensed God was going to receive glory through this impossible situation.

An hour later, back he went to the Commander's office, and pleasantly asked the messenger to go in again and request the permits. He did, and this time came back with two stamped passes!

Hubert hurried home, found the two strongest men, and told them to get the water cart. As they went out the gate he showed the guard the passes. This man hadn't heard the order forbidding the cart, so nodded permission, and they were able to get all the water they needed, then and later.

When this army pulled out, they tried to set fire to the city. The horrified mission community looked out to see the buildings on their north and west sides already burning. As Hubert rushed to the building on the north, a company of Japanese soldiers was passing, so he motioned the officer to come into the building. The latter stopped his men and went in. As Hubert pointed to the fire, the officer stamped on some burning fragments, then hurried away. Hubert immediately took this to mean they could put the fires out, so he called to all the refugees to come and help. A few Chinese from outside also came. They fought the fires all day, and succeeded in putting most of them out.

In appreciation for this heroic venture, a plaque was given to the church by the mayor who had previously fled to the countryside. To the Fishers it was no coincidence, but clearly the overruling of God, that the one officer Hubert had met had signified permission to stop the fires which other officers had ordered.

Chapter 13

A BUSY INTERLUDE AND SOME BAD NEWS

It was fairly quiet for a while after that army left, and the Fishers and Chinese Christian leaders took advantage of this.

For months there had been no mail service in or out; this the missionaries naturally missed very much. At last, on February 1, 1939, Mary was able to write to their prayer partners telling about their situation, and also describing in some detail the kind of work they would be engaged in for most of their remaining time in China.

"During the last two or three weeks we have had something like normal mails again. It has been good to hear from so many of you, and to read of your increased prayer for us. We had felt we were being in a special way upheld, even before you told us so . . . .

"The last circular from my husband was written while he was away, and (unknown to him) while our city was experiencing another invasion, lasting a week. On December 15 seven bombs were dropped outside our compound wall. One of them killed one of the only 15 inhabitants now left in the city, apart from those on our premises.

"During the past months we have had some narrow escapes, but the fact that the Lord has protected us all through, assures us we are where He wants us.

"I'm writing from a city two days journey from home, where I have come for two maternity cases. The morning Miss Finney and I left home cannon firing on two sides of the city began, continuing intermittently all day. There has been no opportunity of knowing what are the circumstances for Hubert and those left with him; it is always easier to trust the Lord for oneself than for others, but He has been showing me that is very imperfect faith.

"Although many of our plans have had to be changed, it has been possible to carry on class work in the city or country during the greater part of these last months. That air raid came in the middle of a month's course of classes taught by Miss Lu and myself, but only one returned home through fear. Only about 30 had come, many being fearful of living in a deserted city.

"One of the courses was 24 lessons on Genesis. Those on Jacob and Joseph especially encouraged some of the younger Christians who are finding the way hard. Each evening we had several tell the Bible stories they had heard during the day. On the whole I was amazed at the clearness with which they told the stories; some occasionally would turn it into a personal testimony, showing that the Lord was applying it to the heart.

"At the close of that month's course, Pastor Yang held a 10-day class for older Christians, with over 40 attending. His messages are always a blessing, for not only is he an excellent Bible teacher, but also puts himself into his message. (Please pray for his health, for he seems on the verge of a breakdown like my husband had. Some days his head is so tired, he cannot read even one verse of Scripture.)

"The evening meeting each day was a class in homiletics, conducted by Miss Lu and Hubert, the object being to help those who want to give voluntary help in preaching in the villages, but have no idea how to go about it . . . All felt this class was a great help.

"After that finished, Miss Lu and I, and two younger Christian women went to work in the villages. At the end of 12 days our work was suddenly brought to a stop by the approach of the Japanese, but not before three had joined the ranks of the King of Kings . . . ." Last came the following significant paragraph:

"Hubert has spent a good deal of time away from home, visiting and encouraging country Christians in the midst of trials, or speaking at church conferences. May I ask prayer for his health, for although we have been conscious of God's daily enabling, the strain of these days has a cumulative effect which only the strength of the Lord can counteract. We do praise God for the privilege of being here, and proving Him for ourselves, and the Chinese Christians, in each new emergency."

After one Japanese army had departed, some Chinese soldiers came, and rounded up thousands of villagers to tear down the city wall. Their idea was that the Japanese would not dare to live in such a defenceless situation.

The Japanese had a strongly fortified position between the city and the mountain, however, and rumours spread quickly that the Chinese were preparing for a big offensive on the plain between the two.

Contrary to expectations, more Japanese troops did come into the city, and this time decided that the missionary compound, and the Fishers' home, would be the safest place for the General and his staff until the battle! In spite of Hubert's strong protests, he and Mary were forced to move to another room on the compound.

The battle was not long in coming, and raged all day. The carnage was horrible, both sides losing heavily. Finally the Japanese artillery, hiding in the city, turned the tide. The Chinese survivors returned to their hideouts in the mountains, and that was their last attempt to retake Yicheng.

Just one incident helped to ease the horror of this battle. Among the carts bringing loads of wounded into the city was one Chinese soldier. The Japanese doctor gave him as careful attention as the others, then sent him back to his village, not far away. The people there had always steadily resisted the Gospel. When this soldier finally limped home, everyone was astonished.

"That doctor must have been a Christian," they all declared. "Only a Christian would care for an enemy in need, and send him home in peace." The doctor was in fact a Christian, and his action resulted in that whole village becoming open to the Gospel.

From that time Yicheng remained quiet, with a permanent Japanese garrison stationed there. They were anxious to pacify the district, and everyone, including the refugees at the mission, were free to come and go. This meant that the gate had to be opened and shut for them from morning till night. Some had left, but there were still over 60 there. Several times the Fishers and Miss Lu suggested they could all leave safely now, and should return home. Some did, but others just smiled and stayed where they were.

"You know, some don't intend to leave until the war's over," Miss Lu said.

"What on earth can we do?" Mary asked in despair.

"We've asked them three times to go. There's nothing more *we* can do," Hubert answered. "We'll just have to leave it to the Lord to get them out."

It was just after that, that news came of World War II starting in Europe. This was certainly going to complicate things in China.

A few days later Hubert returned from some meetings in the

country to find the front gate unlocked, and the big compound completely deserted, except for Mary.

"What in the world has happened?"

"A Christian from Chuwu came rushing over with a message that the British are sending a plane to a nearby area to evacuate all foreigners," Mary explained. "Of course, when the people heard that, they all panicked, thinking we would be going, and left at once."

"Of all things! God certainly knew how to get them out, didn't He! That can't be true. Why should the British come? *We* aren't at war with Japan."

"I shouldn't think it's true," Mary agreed. "But there's hardly anyone left in the city now. Kathleen Heath is alone at Chuwu now that her partner has gone on furlough. They still have 400 refugees in their compound, and she just can't cope with all the opportunities. Miss Lu has gone to help. What do you think about us going over for a time?"

"A great idea! There's certainly nothing left here. Let's go tomorrow, then no one will be tempted to come back here to live."

They hired a handcart to take their bit of luggage, and rode off on their bicycles to Chuwu. They had only been there a few days, however, when they received a letter from two women missionaries at Fencheng, 15 miles west, saying they both had to go to Peking for medical treatment, and could Hubert go and help there until their return.

Accordingly he cycled over and stayed a week, at the end of which he returned to Chuwu to "see how the girls were getting along."

He found them all very happy and extremely busy. But he also learned that Japan was now an acknowledged ally of Germany.

This led the Japanese in China to try to start anti-western feeling there. Some of the men told him it had already begun in Chuwu. In fact some of the refugees were getting nervous, wondering how long the foreigners would stay.

Hubert called the missionaries together to discuss the matter.

"With the Japanese in firm control right from the east coast, and now all this anti-foreign propaganda, don't you think it is time we considered moving into Free China?"

"But there's so much more to do here," protested Kathleen, "and there seems no sign of any danger for us yet."

Mary agreed. "We are having so many encouragements; the

76

people are so responsive. But how are you feeling, Hubert? Have you had any return of your old trouble?"

"No, no. I'm O.K. But the men here seem really concerned."

"Well, why don't you return to Fencheng and keep praying about it? If you really think then it's God's will for us to go, come and tell us," Mary said, and Kathleen agreed.

No sooner was Hubert back in Fencheng than he got down on his knees to pray. Immediately a strange sense of foreboding came over him, and he concluded God was saying, "Get out." So he cycled back the 15 miles to Chuwu, planning they should all leave in a few days.

When he broke the news to the women he was greeted with cries of, "Oh, no! We can't leave yet. The work is going too well," and they hurried off to a meeting.

The usually even-tempered Hubert felt really provoked with them for ignoring what he believed was clear guidance. His anger simmered all the next day, and the following morning, Sunday, he decided to cycle back to Fencheng, although he had made other arrangements for the services there.

Inwardly pouting, he peddled along for half an hour. Then, suddenly, there was what appeared to be a cloud burst. He was soaked immediately, and the short-cut he had taken through the wheat fields became a sea of sticky mud. His temper cooled at once. It was impossible to go on, and he concluded God was sending him back.

So a very wet missionary, carrying a mud-caked bike, appeared at Chuwu just before their morning service. Mary always welcomed his return, but what would she say this time, he wondered.

"Oh, Hubert, how glad I am you're back! God surely has answered prayer. But what a mess you're in. Come and change into dry clothes while I tell you what has happened."

Thankfully dropping his muddy bike, Hubert followed her to their room. "Well, what is it?" he asked.

"You know the city mayor is the brother of one of the elders? Well, he confided to him that he's had orders from the Japanese to hound the foreigners out. Some of the town riff-raff are to break our windows, others to lead an anti-foreign movement against us, thus forcing us to move. The mayor said he could perhaps stall for three days, but no longer."

"Whew! Now I know why the Lord sent the rain to turn me back."

77

Mary picked up his mud-soaked clothes, wondering if they would ever wash clean again.

"Kathleen thought perhaps we could go up into the nearby mountains for a month or two, then things may settle again. The Japanese are afraid to venture up there, and there are lots of villages needing the Gospel."

Hubert said nothing. While he admired the courage of the ladies, he was still convinced they should go to Free China.

After the church service, the elders took them aside, and begged them to leave, lest the church itself suffer through their presence. They hoped it would not be for long.

Early that evening there was a knock at the gate. It was a messenger from the mayor. "There will be an escort of soldiers at 9 a.m. tomorrow, to take you to the station to catch the train for Peking," he announced.

"Peking! That's the very *last* place we want to go," groaned Hubert, as soon as the messenger had gone. "And —why, we could be interned there for the duration of the war!"

Chapter 14

ESCAPE TO THE WEST

The rest of the day and most of the night they hurriedly packed the things they wanted to take, and the things which had to be left in a safe place. The Fishers hadn't brought much from Yicheng, so it looked as if everything left there would be lost. But they helped pack away much of the stuff at Chuwu. Medical supplies were put in the attic; then paper was pasted across the ceiling to conceal the opening. Chinaware went in a big earthenware water barrel which Hubert buried under a rosebush.

The ladies had already packed a supply of jam and other heavy food stuffs for living up in the mountains, and these and other things were made up into carrying pole loads. Hubert piled these near the gate, wondering how they would get them out of the city. If they were forced to go to Peking, they couldn't take them all on the train; the Japanese had commandeered all the carts; if coolies could be got, all this would attract too much attention. It was a problem only God could solve, he thought.

The Chinese pastor was out early next morning to look for carriers, and to his amazement saw a man driving an empty cart. On enquiry, he learned the man had brought in a load of coal for the Japanese, and was now returning empty. He could hardly believe it.

At the mission home they quickly filled the cart with the most important things, covered it with straw, and told the man to take it to the home of a church elder, a day's journey west. He must leave by the north gate through which he entered the city, however, and hope the sentry would recognize him and let him pass without examining the cart. As the missionaries watched it rumble away, they wondered if they would ever see their things again.

They ate a hurried breakfast, had prayer with the church leaders, and then waited almost breathlessly for nine o'clock to strike. Most Chinese were not time-conscious, and the missionaries had decided if the escort hadn't appeared at nine, they would leave immediately by the west gate, heading for freedom.

The last stroke sounded, and Hubert peered up and down the street. No escort was in sight, so leisurely pushing their bicycles, and carrying nothing but lunch baskets, they approached the west gate. Near the gate they thought it best to put on a carefree air, and even joke with each other. The Japanese sentry smiled, and called out the word for "food," evidently thinking they were going for a picnic. They laughingly repeated the word, and added "anniversary," for it was July 11, the Fishers' wedding date.

People were not allowed to ride past a Japanese sentry, but once they were out of his sight they joyfully mounted their bikes and sped off westward. God had wonderfully seen them through this first stage. How many more miracles would be needed before they could settle down to work again, they wondered.

They reached the elder's house after an uneventful journey, and were thankful to find their belongings already unloaded there. The elder welcomed them, but was obviously relieved to hear they would be moving on next morning, and went to hire carriers.

At daybreak they set off on their bikes again, buoyed by the thought that within an hour they would be at the river which at present was the border of the nightmare land of Japanese soldiers. Across it they would be in Free China!

Soon they saw the shining ribbon stretched out in the distance. "What if I do have to wade through water up to my chest," thought Hubert, "this river is flowing into Free China!" His eyes warmed with affection.

A shock greeted them at the water's edge. The cloud burst which had soaked Hubert two days before had resulted in a badly swollen river, quite impossible to ford. The only other crossings were bridges guarded by Japanese soldiers.

Disconsolately they all sat down to rest, and the coolies said they should go back a short distance to an inn, for it would be impossible to cross that day. They decided to stay there for a while, however, hoping a miracle would happen. Hubert thought of the Israelites' crossing of the Jordan. "God's just the same today, and here's our opportunity to prove it," he said.

While the coolies grumbled, the missionaries sat with eyes glued to the river.

"Look! That rock wasn't visible before!" exclaimed Hubert. "It must be going down."

By 9 a.m. the amazed carriers decided they could cross. First they went with all the loads, and bikes held high above their heads, then carried the ladies on their backs, while Hubert, carrying his bike, gradually waded across, his heart singing.

Wet but rejoicing, they were in Free China at last! They thanked God then, and even more later when they heard that in two hours the river had risen again, and couldn't be forded there for nearly two months.

They had heard there was an elderly Christian in a village near the river, so they went to find him. He told them that having come from the Japanese-held area, they could not travel into Free China without a pass from the military forces guarding the frontier. Also they should leave as soon as possible, since there were sometimes people spying for the Japanese. However, the military headquarters, where they must get the pass, was up a mountain not on their route.

"You stay here and keep out of sight," Hubert said to the ladies, "and I'll go up and get the pass."

As he climbed the rocky path he became painfully aware his Chinese cloth shoes were wearing thin. He located the colonel, with some difficulty, and told him his story. Then the officer said, "I was wounded a few months ago, and was nursed back to health in one of your Mission's hospitals. I am glad to help you." He immediately wrote out a pass.

Hubert returned to learn their way ahead was over mountains where their bikes would be useless, and they must hire mules for the ladies and baggage. Hubert as usual would walk, but what about his shoes?

Another old Christian man had heard they were there, and came and insisted on escorting them a short distance. Hubert was really touched when he stopped at last and said, "I see your shoes are worn right through. Here, change with me." With that he removed his almost new shoes, and incredibly they fit Hubert's foreign feet which were larger than the normal Chinese foot.

The second night they came to a village where they had heard there were Christians. The Japanese had reached it once, and left it in ruins before retreating back across the river. Then Chinese soldiers had been billeted there, and in fact had just left that very day. They found the church nothing but a shell, but since there were still some Christians, the travellers decided to stay a few days to encourage them.

They improvised beds and a table from old bricks scattered around the church. There were no doors left on the building, but in one room where there was a mud cooking stove they found a door lying on the floor. So they put all their baggage in that room, and at night propped the door where it belonged. This door wouldn't keep a cat out if it pushed against it, Hubert thought; so he hid a tin can in such a way that if the door moved, the can would crash down and hopefully scare away the intruder. Sure enough, this happened two nights later. Hubert jumped up in time to see a man fleeing through the front door opening.

A few mornings later Hubert was hurrying to leave to visit Christians in Hen Town, 20 miles west, when Mary called him.

"Could you please move this box for me before you go?"

Hubert grabbed it, then gasped, "Oh! My back!" He just managed to crawl to his bed on the bricks, and lay there on his back for a week. Even when the district mayor visited them he couldn't turn on his side to greet him.

The seventh morning as he lay feeling sorry for himself, and wondering if the Japanese might not return again, a verse came to his mind: "You have not because you ask not." What a lovely verse, he thought, as he savoured it in his mind. Then it struck him: "Isn't this God speaking to me?" He was convinced it was. So he prayed for healing, rolled on his side, got out of bed, and walked to Hen Town without discomfort.

On the way he saw a column of Chinese soldiers marching towards him and his companions. Hubert hastily pulled out a bunch of the tracts he always carried, ready to give to them.

At their head was the colonel, riding a horse. When Hubert held out a tract, he stopped, and all the men halted behind him. When he saw what it was he dismounted, thanked Hubert, and told him he had recently become a Christian.

"I went into the church in Hen Town," he said, "just to see what a Christian worship place was like, and was surprised to see no idols, just a text on the wall which really struck me."

"What was it?" Hubert asked.

" 'Father, forgive them, for they know not what they do.' The preacher explained about God sending His own Son, and the agony and death He endured to be our Saviour. Then and there I prayed, and put my trust in Christ."

Hubert joyfully gave away all his tracts, thanking God for healing him at the right time to meet this new Christian and encourage him to witness to his men.

Soon they headed for Sian, the capital of Shensi province, a journey that took them two months to complete, and included crossing the great Yellow River. Of the many memorable experiences during this time one incident must suffice here.

They arrived early one afternoon at the town where they were to spend the night. As Hubert walked down the main street, whom should he meet but the medical student who had accepted Christ the first time the Japanese advanced on Yicheng.

He was delighted to see Hubert, and took him to the medical college, which had relocated there. It had mud walls, mud stove, mud desks and seats, but classes went on as usual. Hubert was invited to address the students on the topic, "What is a Christian?"

Mary summarized their experiences in a circular dated November 29, 1939.

"We do praise God 1) for all His protection on the journey, sometimes in rain, in intense heat, and over very difficult mountain roads. 2) for help in time of sickness, [Hubert's back; Kathleen's appendicitis; Mary's dysentery, which was so bad that she had to be carried by stretcher]. 3) For the joy of service in places where no foreigner has been for years, and we were so warmly welcomed. 4) For the supply of all our need. As you realize, we were not at our own station when the trouble arose; so for the second time in less than two years we have lost most of our possessions. But friends have been very kind in sharing their things . . . .

"The last two years have seen unusual opportunities in Shansi, in spite of all the fighting, and many have been added to the church. We hear they are now facing persecution, and two have been martyred, while others are living in caves. Our former premises are occupied by the military . . . ." It was not a pleasant picture; and what might lie ahead?

Chapter 15

A NEW HOME

Even when the Fishers finally reached Sian, they hadn't entirely escaped the Japanese. After their first breakfast, air raid sirens sounded, and everyone fled outside the city and watched while a factory was bombed and burned. A few days later word came from the Mission, asking them to go to Meihsien. They had the luxury of travelling seven hours by train to this city. It had a well-established church with 360 members, but 200 of these attended branch churches in villages. It was amongst these that the Fishers would work.

During their first year there, they received a letter from missionaries in Sian saying their former neighbour across the mountains from Yicheng, Gladys Aylward, was in hospital there, very sick. Mary thought they should go to see her. While they were at the station five miles away, waiting for a train, Rueben Gustafson drove up, and introduced himself as a member of the Scandinavian Alliance Mission in Sian.

"You better go home at once," he said. "We broke open your window, and have put Gladys Aylward in your bed! She couldn't stand the strain of the sirens and bombings in Sian, though she was having the best of care at the Baptist hospital. So Nurse Nelson and I brought her down here."

From then on Mary had to drop all other work and care for Gladys from morning to night for six months.

The Japanese had put a price on her head, and she had managed to escape to Free China with 80 orphans. By the time she reached Sian she had four diseases, typhus, relapsing fever, pneumonia and dysentery. In her very weak condition the bombings were driving her to hysteria, and the only hope of maintaining her mental balance was to be in a quiet place. She recovered and her story is well known through books and a film.

In addition to her, 200 other refugees from the east fled to the district, and Hubert was able to get relief funds to help them start farms on land provided by the county. Many of these became Christians, and eventually the four central churches of the area increased to 22, mainly as a result of Japan's invasion.

Soon after their arrival in Meihsien, Mary had told the church leaders about the week-long classes she had held for women in Shansi. So they invited her to do the same there, arranging the first at a market town about 10 miles away. Shortly before she was to leave, Mary realized to her great joy that after eight years of marriage she was at last pregnant. Not wanting to disappoint the women at this very first class by staying home to rest, she decided to hire a donkey to ride, instead of walking. Unfortunately this resulted in a miscarriage the next day. In her usual sweet spirit Mary wrote home that "the joy which came as a result of the response of the women to the teaching more than compensated for our loss." In fact it had drawn the women to her in loving concern.

The Fishers had not been long in Meihsien when an order went out from the city office that all opium smokers were to stop within a month, or face severe punishment. There had never been such a law before, and about 500 addicts went to the city hall for treatment, while 120 responded to the invitation of the Christians to come to the church for help. There they were told the Gospel, and taught to pray and sing choruses. After 10 days they left, saying they were cured.

Hubert and another Christian went to visit them a month later to see how they were doing, and found many had returned to opium. Evidently the mass treatment had not worked so well as the individual attention Hubert had given in Kweichow. When they came to one village, however, some people saw them and said, "We know who you have come to see. They are cured all right!" They then led them to the home of a middle-aged couple.

The pair welcomed them warmly, and invited them to sit on the only bench, while they sat on the bed and listened to what the visitors had to teach them. Just as it began to get dusk, they suddenly both bounded off the bed, and rushed outside.

Hubert followed in amazement. They went to the furthest corner of the garden, prayed at the top of their voices, then returned and sat on the bed, looking expectantly for the visitors to continue.

"You don't need to yell your head off when you talk to God," Hubert remonstrated, "He isn't deaf. Nor need you go outside—"

"Yes, we know," they interrupted, "but it's like this. We

were both very bad cases—real slaves to opium—and at the church there were so many people we just got away as far as we could to pray. There was so much noise there we just *had* to pray loudly. But God heard our prayers and delivered us from opium, and made us His children. So having got used to praying that way, we continued when we got home."

Hubert said no more.

He and Mary had spent two or three very happy and fruitful years in Meihsien when the Mission asked them to move to Fengsiang, a much more needy place 25 miles further west. They were sad to leave, but faced this new challenge with their usual willingness and courage. Mercifully they had no knowledge of all the difficulties and dangers they would meet there.

They had moved so much during this second term of service they hardly dared to feel settled anywhere, but Fengsiang turned out to be their base over a span of 10 years. Of course, both of them spent weeks at a stretch away teaching classes, and holding conferences. Also, after eight and a half years service, they took furlough in 1945, after Japan was defeated. In addition there was to be a memorable evacuation involving separations, uncertainties, and great physical hardships. At first, however, it was peaceful, and they set about getting to know the church and their neighbors.

In the next street lived a fierce-looking medical officer in the Chinese army, a major Ma, whose wife's nerves were very bad. She began attending church, and the day came when she received pardon and peace through Christ.

Hubert first saw the husband one day when he had gone at 7 a.m. to preach to wounded soldiers billeted in a local temple. The doctor came to see his patients, and eyed Hubert, too, but did not speak to him. Later in the day he strolled up to Hubert's office, however.

"I want to buy a Bible," he announced in a gruff voice.

Hubert invited him in and showed him several. When he had chosen one, Hubert smiled and said, "Excuse my asking, but why do you want a Bible?"

"There has been a great change in my wife since she's been coming to the church."

"And what about yourself?"

"Oh, I'm all right."

"In that case we can't help you," Hubert explained in a kindly voice. "You see, Jesus said He was like a doctor, and that well people don't need a doctor, only the sick. If there is nothing that needs to be changed in your life, then Christ can't help you."

At that, Major Ma sat down with a thoughtful expression.

"Well," he finally said, "My mother-in-law lives with us. I don't treat her as I should."

"You can start with that then," Hubert said encouragingly. "Why not kneel down and confess that to the Lord?"

The proud officer knelt at his chair, and began to confess that sin. Then all the liquor he drank daily came to his mind. Gradually many other things were confessed. Finally he accepted forgiveness, and went out trusting Christ. He walked home, went straight to the cupboard where he kept his drink, and poured it all out. From then on he attended church regularly as long as he was stationed there.

Major General Liu, another officer Hubert met there, had first been stationed 10 miles from the city. There he received fresh recruits for training. Sometimes they came from far away, and often were so badly crowded in railway boxcars there were nearly always some dead on arrival. One day while he was worrying about this problem, one of his captains dropped in and during their conversation told the General his mother-in-law, a Christian, was visiting them.

"She keeps urging me to become a Christian," he added. "She says they always have peace of heart, and aren't afraid to die."

"Do Christians have some clue about death?" queried the General. "Ask your mother-in-law to come over and have a chat."

Later that day when the officer reported this to his mother-in-law her response was, "I'm too ignorant a person to talk to the General, but when I return home I'll ask our preacher to go and talk to him."

A few days later the preacher showed up at the General's headquarters, and was kindly received. He couldn't answer some of the General's questions, so he said, "General, I haven't the education or brains that you have. I cannot argue with you, but if you have any personal problems, I can show you how to solve them."

Do I have anything *but* problems, Liu thought to himself.

"Well," he began, "I'm an inveterate gambler, and my temper is so bad that when my children see me coming home, they run and hide."

Having heard that honest confession, the preacher knew how to help him.

"You must pray to God, confess those and any other sins; then God will forgive and change you. He can do it because of the sacrifice of Christ on the cross for you."

The worried General knelt down and poured out his heart to God. He trusted Christ as his Saviour, and got up a changed man. At once he set off for home. Seeing him back at that time of day his wife was really scared, but he spoke kindly to her and the children. He told them of his conversion, and finished with the words, "You never need to be afraid of me again."

Shortly after that he moved into the city, and invited Hubert and the church leaders to have open air meetings standing on the veranda in front of his house. He would come out and his wife would stand beside him, with a baby in her arms.

"Before my husband became a Christian," she would call out to the crowd, "our home was hell on earth. Now it is like heaven." And he would nod in agreement.

After being a Christian for a short time other things began to bother his conscience. One Sunday in church he told the congregation that in a battle with the Japanese once, he had become so scared, he shot himself in the leg, and had to be carried off the field. It must have taken great courage to confess such a thing, but he not only did it in church, but also wrote a letter to his commanding officer about it. He expected to be severely punished and demoted, but instead, after a few weeks he was promoted as commander over all the forces in the army in the far northwest of China.

It was here that Mao and his Red Army had been hiding, and as soon as Japan was defeated they aimed to take control of the whole country. Already some distant areas were being threatened into submission, while many people were swallowing Red Army propaganda from secret agents everywhere. Unknown to the Fishers, some of the latter were already among their contacts in Fengsiang.

Chapter 16

THE RED GRIP TIGHTENS

Soon after the Fishers returned from furlough, refugees once more began arriving from the east where the Reds were now in control. Among them were Ian and Helen Anderson who now taught in the Bible school that Mr. and Mrs. J. H. Taylor II had started in the Fengsiang compound. It now had 25 students and some Chinese teachers helping.

Some of the stories the refugees told were horrible. A former kind neighbor of the Fishers', a wealthy farmer, had been brought before a public tribunal by the Communists, and people were urged to tell how he had harmed them. There was silence, until finally a woman said her chicken had strayed on his land and he had killed it. The officials then calculated the cost of all the possible eggs hatched in the years since, which came to more than the man owned. The man was executed, and all the money put in the party coffers, not shared with the woman.

It was good to hear that many Christians were standing firm in faith in face of persecution, however, and one story was specially encouraging. Many churches had been ordered to close. In one such place the wife of the Communist official became very sick and no doctor could help her. She finally insisted her husband call the pastor of the church to pray for her. She was obviously dying, and fearing her spirit would torment him, the husband reluctantly agreed. Several Christians came and prayed, and immediately she was healed. As a result, the church was allowed to reopen.

This man was soon replaced, however, and a higher official sent who again closed the church. His wife then became very sick, and hearing what had happened to her predecessor, she asked her husband to send for the Christians. This was a bitter pill, but he had paid a large sum for his wife, and also feared her spirit if she died; so he finally gave in. She was healed, too, and again the church was able to re-open.

A wealthy Chinese Christian in Shensi, planning to move to

the safety of Szechuan province, now offered to lend the Bible School some larger premises he owned in Paoki, a city at the end of the railway line to the south west of Fengsiang. They therefore gladly moved from their crowded quarters, leaving the Fishers alone in the Fengsiang compound.

Meanwhile the Communists continued to gain ground, though still far from Fengsiang. It was assumed that if they ever came it would be to Sian first, in the east, so there would be plenty of warning. But one day, just after Hubert had left for the country, Mary got word that the Reds were approaching from the north, only 60 miles away. By now there was a telephone system; so Mary was kept busy notifying the Superintendent, Percy Moore, and alerting all missionaries to the east. Percy decided all should proceed south to Nancheng where he lived. Next day was the usual business of packing, packing away, and hiring carts. Mary was very glad to see Hubert back that evening.

When their carts had not arrived by 6 a.m. Hubert went to look for them, but was back in a few minutes.

"The Reds are only 10 miles away! The city gates are to be opened in a few minutes to let everyone out; then they'll block them with sandbags. Our carts have all been commandeered!"

So Hubert rushed Mary off with the cook, who, with a bundle on his back was to ride a bike Hubert had borrowed from another missionary, while Mary carried what she could on the five mile walk to the station. Rain poured down all the way. It took seven hours to wade through thick mud, the bicycle having to be carried. Hubert didn't catch up with them until evening, and they were fortunate to be given a tiny space in a boxcar of a military evacuation train, reaching Paoki at 2 a.m. Again they had to travel separately, with various adventures, but finally reached Nancheng.

There they found 40 people of different missions gathered in the crowded compound. Most decided to go to Szechuan province where Chiang Kai Shek was still in control, but the Fishers decided to return to Fengsiang when they heard the Reds did not stay there long. They had only been back a short time, however, when Hubert was asked to be acting Superintendent in Nancheng, to relieve the Moores for a much needed furlough.

In spite of their many recent stresses and hardships, Mary was able to write to their prayer partners on September 15, 1948:

"Be prepared for a shock. There should be an addition to our family next March! . . ." Twice she nearly lost it, and was ordered to stay in bed for two months. To her parents she wrote: "We are staying with Mr. and Mrs. Malins, the latter a nurse; so I have had excellent care. Now I am somewhat better; I teach the Sunday School Teachers' Preparation Class from my bed, and help Mrs. Malins prepare messages for the Women's Prison."

In spite of all the care, something was wrong.

"Day and night my heart was filled with joy and love," Mary wrote, "but it was not to be. Again the dreaded symptoms appeared. I continued to hope when there was not hope. But as the hours dragged on (with no medical help) and I became increasingly weak, it began to dawn on me that it was God who had allowed this . . . He was asking me to give back to Him what had become my most prized possession. I thought of how unstintingly He had given His beloved Son to be my Saviour. Then how could I keep anything from Him, even that I had wanted most? I realized it was His prerogative to take, but my privilege to give, *gladly*. And so, after a struggle, with utter abandon to His will I prayed, 'I now joyfully give to You that which You have loaned to me for this short time, and which has brought me much joy. Because You ask, I gladly give.'

"Although tears were rolling down my cheeks, my heart was filled with a joy I can't describe. Now I could only think of our precious little one with Jesus. I asked Hubert to sing over and over, 'Safe in the arms of Jesus, safe on His gentle breast,' and my heart was comforted. I had given my dearest to Him, and He Himself had become far more precious to me."

There can be no doubt that hundreds of women in China, and some in Japan would never have found Christ if Mary had not been free from home responsibilities to give herself unsparingly to serve the Saviour she loved so dearly. Many Chinese house-churches today are in areas the Fishers worked in, and often their leaders are women.

While many missions left the country as early as 1948, when the Reds had seized some areas, it seemed at first that it was only the landowners and wealthy whom the Communists treated harshly. They even put up notices on temples and some churches, "Religious Freedom." The CIM were therefore unwilling to leave. The Fishers' area had not yet been 'liberated'; so they certainly wished to continue, and thus returned to Paoki to help in the Bible school.

One day the Nationalist army was in the city, and the next there was a battle outside, leaving the Reds in control, but everything continued as usual. After a month however, it was discovered that the Bible school did not own the property, but that it was owned by a rich Chinese. From then on it seemed wiser to return to Fengsiang. The Red officials played a cat and mouse game, ten times agreeing to let them go, only to turn them back at the city gate. The imperturbable Hubert went cheerfully the eleventh time, and they got through.

They were warmly welcomed back by the Christians in Fengsiang, but soon there were various forms of harassment to give concern.

One day two Red cadres (their name for leaders or officials) came to see Hubert, and haughtily denounced him for preaching religion and deceiving the people.

He happened to be standing beside a wall on which was a large poster of "The Two Roads." Seeing the cadres' eyes on the many bad things depicted on the broad road leading to destruction, Hubert at once seized the opportunity to explain the whole poster, showing them Christ on the cross, and declaring that He is the *only* way to the right road.

"Why do you say that?" snapped one angrily.

"I'm telling you the *facts*," Hubert replied with a smile. "I could introduce you to 200 ex-opium addicts in this area. They will all tell you that until they prayed for forgiveness and help from Christ they couldn't break free. How do you plan to help opium smokers?"

"Kill them off. We'll give them one month to get unhooked, and if they're still smoking, we'll kill them," answered one.

"I think the Christian way is better. You kill them; we reform them and make them good producers," Hubert declared.

Nonplussed, their arrogance melted. "You continue that work," one muttered.

The Andersons had been away for dental work. While they were there, the city where the dentist lived was "liberated" so it was some months before they were allowed to leave. A few days after their return to Fengsiang, two policemen called and said they had to take Hubert and Ian to the police station for questioning.

The Fishers and Andersons were the only foreigners in the city. Judging others by their own practices, the Communists assumed that they were really spies, preaching religion as a "front." So they planned now to interrogate them thoroughly, to prove that they were spies.

Feeling full of joy at this opportunity to test Christ's words in Mark 13:11, "When they take you away to hand you to the authorities, don't worry beforehand what you will say," the two men stepped out so briskly that the shorter policemen had to almost trot to keep up with them.

They were led to a room with eight Red officers facing them in a semi-circle, and were told to sit.

Hubert describes Ian as "an exceedingly innocent-looking person" who would thus make an ideal spy. Perhaps for this reason they questioned him first.

"What's your name? education? your father's work?" and so on. There were to be 30 questions, most of which could be answered without thinking. Then came the 28th.

"When you left China last time, how did you travel?"

"By plane," he replied.

The inquisitors all seemed to move to the edge of their seats and rivet their eyes on Ian as the next question was snapped at him.

"Did you pay for your ticket?"

"I certainly did," groaned Ian. "Four hundred and eighty British pounds! That was too much, don't you think?" he added, as though hoping for sympathy.

They nodded, but their expression implied, what do you expect from capitalists. Their last two questions were inconsequential. Certainly Anderson wasn't a spy, they concluded, or he wouldn't have had to pay his fare.

It was Hubert's turn. The questions were identical. At last came No. 28.

"Last time you left China, how did you travel out?"

Now the Fishers had left right after the end of the war, when there was no public transportation. They had travelled from north to central China courtesy of one U.S. military plane; to south-west China on another; and over the Himalayan 'Hump' to India on another, without paying a cent! Certainly this could incriminate him in their eyes, but he had no intention of lying.

"By plane," he answered firmly.

Forgetting the second half of that question they went straight on to 29 which Hubert answered with an enthusiasm which surprised them! Now clear of suspicion, the missionaries were dismissed, and for a time were able to move freely. Once again

God had shown His power and His glory.

One church in a neighbouring place had always held a week's summer conference. This year they applied to the new Red official for permission, and were curtly told religious conferences were a thing of the past. When they dolefully told Hubert this, he felt he should encourage them to plan one, and invite the police chief.

Hubert was asked to lead a congregation of about 400 in prayer the second morning. Hearing some movement in front, he squinted with one eye, and saw the police chief standing not a foot away from him. He closed that eye in a hurry!

After the prayer, the police chief was invited to the pulpit to have his say. He had brought along the Worker's Newspaper, which had evidently just come in the mail, and had an article headed, "How We at this Stage should Treat Religions," and he evidently thought this would be suitable. As he read, however, he was obviously surprised and began to stumble in his reading when it stated that the authorities should "tread gently in the beginning." Of course he had to allow the meetings to continue, and others hearing this were encouraged to hold their conferences. Thus many were able to have a real feast in God's word—for the last time.

Chapter 17

GOD OF IMPOSSIBLE PLUSES

By the next year the Communists were in control everywhere, and their attitude hardened. Soon, every prominent tree, post and fence were hung with lurid anti-American posters. Many churches were now closed, and the Fishers were refused permission to travel. They still did some teaching in the Bible School, but the curriculum had to be curtailed for more "productive" things such as stocking-knitting, tailoring, bee-keeping and vegetable growing. Hubert took his turn pasturing the goats.

Fewer students registered in September '50, and conditions were very cramped as 'others' (i.e. local communists) were occupying some dormitory and classroom space. Mary wrote early in '51, "Our living room is now a classroom, and inconvenient for us as our bedroom opens onto it, and we don't like to disturb classes."

Christians everywhere were threatened, and told to have nothing to do with "imperialist" foreign missionaries. So the CIM at last regretfully told all their missionaries to apply for permission to leave, for the sake of the Christians.

On February 17, Hubert wrote to his family:

"We are loath to leave this country where we have spent half our lives and have seen God's power and glory in so many ways. We are looking to Him to show us where to go from here. We feel it would be too bad if we don't work among foreigners, since we have spent so much time and thought seeking to know them and to conform ourselves to their ways."

Applying for permission and receiving it were two very different things, however. Some missionaries were imprisoned for a time, and others harassed. When Hubert went to the Bureau of Foreign Affairs in Fengsiang he was told their cases would have to be thoroughly investigated before a visa from Peking would be granted them and the Andersons.

It was four months before the visa came, and then they were told it would only be valid when stamped by the mayor of Paoki, where they were when the Communists took over.

Remembering that it was in Paoki he had had to make eleven trips to the official just to move to Fengsiang, Hubert wondered how much more difficult it would be to get permission to leave the country! As he cycled the four hours to Paoki, his mind was full of foreboding.

He parked his bike at the church, then walked slowly towards the mayor's office. It was a civilian official now, but Hubert didn't feel optimistic that this would make it any easier. These doleful thoughts caused his head to droop, and his steps to drag, as he tried to think of a way to persuade the mayor to grant his request.

About 200 yards from his destination, he noticed a pharmacy he had never seen before, and the proprietor, seeing a foreigner passing, called him in. Glad of an interruption to his unpleasant errand, Hubert walked in.

"Would you like to see this medical book the Communist government has put out?" the man asked.

Hubert took the paper-backed volume, and sat down. The first introduction was by Mao Tse Tung himself. Only half a page long, its message was "All Chinese doctors should have Dr. Norman Bethune as their model." The second introduction, a full page by General Chung Ye, head of the Red Army, was also in praise of Norman Bethune. Marvelling at God's provision, Hubert handed back the book, thanked the owner, and with a new light in his eye walked briskly on to the office, and asked to see the mayor.

The receptionist handed him a magazine, and told him to read the article indicated. It took a whole hour to read, and Hubert learned from it that those whom Jesus spoke of as whited sepulchres, wolves in sheeps clothing, and hypocrites were actually the missionaries in China.

He politely handed it back to the young man, but was given another, and then another article to read. He realized then that the man had no intention of letting him see the mayor.

"Excuse me, did you happen to know Dr. Bethune?"

"Dr. Bethune! I should say I did! He was with us in Yemen," the receptionist cried.

"I am also a Canadian, and from the same province. Could you give me the address of his parents? I would like to tell them how much you Communists appreciated him."

The receptionist shook his head. "But you look them up and tell them how much we appreciated their son. By the way, what is it you want?''

"I wish to see the mayor," Hubert replied, with all the authority befitting one from the same country as Bethune.

"Go through the door," the man said, pointing politely.

Hubert went through, and there, not ten feet away, a burly man was sitting on a little stool in a courtyard. He seemed surprised that anyone had been allowed in, but motioned to a stool opposite, and began a long harangue about the evils of imperialism.

He was interrupted by a man bringing a new pair of cloth shoes for him to try on. It was amusing to watch the big man struggling to do this on the small stool, but he talked non-stop, and by now an hour had passed. At last there was a moment's pause, and Hubert took the plunge.

"Did you know Dr. Norman Bethune?"

The mayor nearly jumped off the stool. "I certainly did! The Canadian Communists sent him out to help us. Alas! he died a few years ago."

"I come from the same province in Canada. Could you give me the address of his parents, so I can visit them, and tell them how much you appreciated their son here?"

"Unfortunately we don't have their address. But you find them and tell them we appreciated him very highly. What do you want, anyway?"

Hubert took the visa from his pocket. "Just your chop on this, please."

The mayor fished in his pocket for his official stamp, and down it came on the visa.

With a light step Hubert returned to his bike and gaily cycled back to Fengsiang.

There was little to pack, for they were leaving most of their possessions to the Bible School. By 10 a.m. next morning they were ready to begin their long journey to Honk Kong, the first leg of which was by train to Sian.

In every possible way the Bible School had tried to fit in with the new regime. They had cut down all the trees in the garden, and dug every foot of ground to grow vegetables. Outwardly they could not fraternize with "enemy" missionaries. On the last morning all the students gathered in the Fishers' dining room, sitting quietly, unable to speak. Since no one seemed in charge, Hubert went to the front to say a few words, but had hardly begun when they all started weeping. Hubert prayed, then he and Mary went out of the door for the last time.

No one dared go to the gate to see them off, but one of the men from the church took a side road, and met them half a mile out of town. He wept as he walked beside them, repeating over and over, "God be with you."

In Sian another big hurdle faced them. Although they had their precious visa with the mayor's stamp, they must also get someone in China to "guarantee" them, before they could leave. The guarantor had to promise that if anyone claimed the departed person owed them money, he would pay without question. Also, if anyone in their zeal for Communism and hatred of imperialism decided to kill the missionary on the way out, the guarantor must be held responsible.

These conditions were so preposterous, Hubert felt quite unable to ask anyone in Fengsiang to undertake such a responsibility. Where in the world would such a person be found? Only God could provide one, Hubert concluded. Now they were actually in Sian, and could not board the main line train south, without this.

Many other missionaries, in the same condition as themselves, were passing through Sian, they discovered. The Scandinavian Alliance Mission, an associate of CIM, had pulled out more than a year before. The church they had left in Sian agreed upon a most courageous and loving gesture, which they would later suffer for. One of their evangelists, who had been greatly helped by missionaries as a child, was to guarantee all from the CIM in the church's name.

The train didn't leave until evening, and Hubert suddenly thought he would visit an old friend from the Bible School, now pastor of the Free Methodist church. During the visit this man mentioned that his mission in Hong Kong had promised them 480 Chinese dollars, but had no way of getting it to them now.

"Could you possibly let me have the money here, and collect the other in U.S. dollars when you get to Hong Kong?" he asked anxiously.

Hubert was delighted. He happened to have nearly 500 Chinese dollars which he would not be allowed to take out of the country, and didn't think he would need on the journey. Thus the needs of both men were happily met.

After all the pressures and difficulties the Fishers and Andersons had been subjected to, they boarded the train with overwhelming relief, thinking mistakenly that all their problems were over. But it was no pleasure trip. The train was crowded, and they had to sit on hard wooden seats all night and all day through sweltering heat.

Consequently when they stopped at a junction in central China to change trains for Canton, Hubert went to the ticket office, and asked,

"Do you happen to have four sleeper tickets?"

"No," was the reply in a tone which suggested if he had, they wouldn't be given to an imperialist enemy.

Disappointed, Hubert turned to see the Andersons and Mary watching an official examining everything in their suitcases. When Hubert got there the official even opened his fountain pen to see if it concealed any secret notes. Nothing incriminating was found.

Next he went through Anderson's things and all was well until he began searching Ian himself. In the first pocket of his jacket was a map of the route they were taking, with several places marked.

"Why do you have this marked map?" he demanded, and wasn't satisfied with Ian's answer.

It was even worse in the other pocket. There he found about 50 pieces of newspaper neatly cut into four-inch squares. All travellers had to carry their own supply of toilet paper then, so that in itself was not suspicious. What *was* incriminating, apparently, was that they were cut from *The London Times*. The official went through them, piece by piece, and saw one with the headline "Communism in the Empire."

"Where did you get that newspaper?"

"It came by post," Ian said.

"When did it come?"

"I don't remember; perhaps six months ago."

"That's contraband! It couldn't have come through the post office, you must have some secret way of getting it in. You are a spy!" So saying, he hurried off with the map and papers to his superior inside. He soon returned.

"You and your wife will be detained here to stand trial!" he snapped.

Oh no! they all felt. *This can't be happening to us!* Mary and Helen sat on a bench and prayed, while Hubert and Ian tried to convince the official Ian wasn't a spy. After arguing for ten minutes they persuaded him to go inside again, and ask if they could get on the train.

"You have to stay!" he announced to the Andersons a few minutes later, "You go," to the Fishers.

The moment of stunned silence which followed was broken by spurting blasts of steam from the Canton train as it prepared to start.

"No, we must stay, too," Mary said, "we are all on the same ticket." She held it out to him.

Grabbing the ticket, he rushed in again, while they waited in an agony of suspense. He reappeared, shouting angrily, "All of you get on the train."

As Mary thankfully snatched the ticket and hurried to the train with the Andersons, common sense should have made Hubert follow them. Instead, he raced to the ticket office again, and asked, "Perhaps now that the train is leaving you have four sleepers free?"

The clerk stared at him in unbelief. "Well, yes, I had four for some important foreign Communist officials, but they haven't arrived. Take them."

Hubert put down the exact money, and tore back to the train just as it was jerking to a start. They found they had first class sleepers, all for the price of four U.S. dollars.

"Now I know why we were held up so long with that cadre," Hubert said with satisfaction, when he got his breath. "If we'd been allowed on the train at once, we'd have had to sit up all night, but by being delayed until the train left we were able to get these sleepers. Surely that was the Lord making it a plus for us." The others, though still badly shaken from their recent ordeal, had to agree.

They enjoyed a good night's sleep, and were up when the train stopped at a station about 6 a.m. Hubert looked out, and was amazed to see about 5,000 high school and university students sitting on the ground looking up at their coach. They were there to greet the four VIP foreign officials whose sleepers the missionaries had occupied.

Hubert immediately went out, smiling and waving. He didn't have time to address the students as the train was about to move, but thought afterwards he could at least have repeated John 3:16 to them.

Arriving in Canton the foreigners were all separated and lined up while a cadre, who only looked about 17, examined their passports and pockets. Once again finding nothing but ink in Hubert's pen they were all passed. Then Hubert noticed a dark-faced burly man next to him take out a rather home-made looking passport with PORTUGUAL on it. The cadre studied it a full moment, then showed it to Hubert.

"What do you think of this? It doesn't look genuine, does it?"

Hubert looked at it carefully, and curled his lip in disdain. "You know, Portugal is a very small country," was all he said.

"Why, of course," the cadre agreed, and handed the passport back to the man. The latter didn't look at Hubert, but later the French Consul's wife thanked him profusely. They were then herded into another room for their luggage to be searched. They found Hubert's books either interesting or suspect, for they were all confiscated. So with lightened luggage, and very light hearts they walked across the bridge to freedom.

Chapter 18

A NEW CHALLENGE

At the end of the bridge was Hong Kong, and missionary friends to welcome them. What a relief it was to be in British-controlled territory!

"Here we need not be so careful to answer a fool according to his folly," Hubert wrote. "In Hong Kong we see the vast differences between a country with laws based on the word of God, and where the Gospel can be freely preached, and a country where laws are based only on men's ideas, and force is used to make people think as the government wishes."

The question now was "Where should we go next?" Mary had experienced noises in her ear for a few months, and Hubert had some eye trouble. They had been back in China five very difficult years, and could have chosen to go home as many others were doing.

"No, we'd like to complete our normal seven-year term," Hubert said, when asked.

"Now that the Mission has decided to work in other countries, it would be best to begin there as soon as possible," Mary added. "Then when we go home we can tell people about it firsthand, and they can pray more intelligently."

They considered Malaysia and the Philippines. Then a team which had been sent to survey the prospects in Japan came and told of the great need they had seen. At once the Fishers were convinced they should go there.

Hubert bought a Japanese grammar, and after studying it only 15 minutes the old pain in his head would return. He was tempted to give up. Yet God had called them to Japan, so he kept quiet, not even telling Mary about it. Later in Japan he found that sitting facing the pleasant Japanese teachers the pain did not return.

They were the first in the Mission to go to Japan, and landing at Yokohama in the summer heat was a testing time. They expected to be met by Julius Bergstrom, an old friend from Sian of the Scandinavian Alliance Mission, now known as T.E.A.M.

They waited four hours, and were trying to get a taxi when he arrived. He had been unavoidably delayed, and had no way of informing them.

"It looks like we'll need plenty of patience in Japan," Hubert said to Mary when they arrived at last at TEAM headquarters in Tokyo, "but everything will turn out all right in the end." His prediction was to prove accurate.

TEAM withdrew from China a year before the C.I.M. and had already established a language school at a wooded mountain resort several hours north of Tokyo by train. Summer villas could be rented cheaply here as the Japanese were still very impoverished after the war. TEAM was glad to share facilities and know-how with the C.I.M., now to be called the Overseas Missionary Fellowship. This was a great help as the Fishers prepared for other OMF workers to join them a month later.

Hubert and Mary were now fifty, and one Japan missionary told them, "Don't expect to get the language at your age; it's very difficult."

"We certainly *do* expect to," Hubert responded characteristically, and in their 20 years in Japan they became more proficient than many younger missionaries. To the latter they were a constant inspiration and challenge. The Japanese, too, remarked on Hubert's wide vocabulary. When they occasionally laughed at mistakes in a sermon he was never embarrassed, but asked afterwards what he had said, so he could avoid repeating it.

A year in language school was considered necessary for everyone, but in their last 2 1/2 months the Fishers were invited to stay with the Bees, veteran missionaries of the Japan Evangelistic Band, working in the south. Here they studied and also saw actual mission work in Japan which was so different from China.

"The Japanese seem more philosophical, and certainly more reserved than the Chinese," Hubert remarked.

"Yes, and Mrs. Bee says their national Shinto religion, which teaches they are all descended from gods, together with Buddhism, makes it hard for them to see themselves as sinners, and so needing Christ," Mary said. "It's going to be hard, I can see."

"It needs an average of 40 visits or contacts before a Japanese is ready to become a Christian," one missionary had told them. Yet at the Bees' they were encouraged by seeing two people accept Christ in that home after much briefer contact.

They were shown a large, needy area where OMF might work, and even had a few potential helpers in mind. Then word came that the Mission had decided to open work in the northern part of Japan.

"What a disappointment," Mary sighed, "but I'm sure they have prayed much about it."

"I can't see how it could be needier than here," Hubert muttered. "But—the Lord can overrule it."

Six single girls were also ready to leave language school, and a Presbyterian missionary, Mr. Chapman, had urged the OMF to go up to the northern island of Hokkaido, saying there were many areas with no Christian witness.

In addition to language, housing was the biggest problem facing new missionaries in Japan then. So much property had been bombed in the war, and the bankrupt country could do little re-building for some years.

Rooms were eventually found for the single girls in two towns, while the Fishers rented one at a lodging house in a fishing village of 6,000 people. Mr. Chapman had recommended it as a place where there were a few Christians who had begged him to live there when he had visited it once.

The Fishers enjoyed getting to know the Christians for a few weeks, until one day the irate Supervisor of the United Church of Japan came from Sapporo, the capital city, to say this was *their* work—although they could only send a preacher once a month from nearly 100 miles away.

The Christian doctor begged the Fishers to stay and start a separate group, but they had no wish to create division and strife, and decided to look elsewhere. It was a disappointing start.

A pleasant looking place called Samani, further down the railway line, had attracted Hubert, but Mr. Street, the new Mission Superintendent for Japan, thought they should go to a larger place further on. He and Hubert went there with an interpreter, but although the mayor was friendly, he couldn't find anywhere for them to live.

"No building has been done since the war," he apologized, "and a recent earthquake unfortunately destroyed 80 houses here."

So they went to Samani. The interpreter tried all the usual channels, again without success. As the three returned to the station around 4 p.m. Hubert suddenly felt he must make one more effort himself. He had 12 tracts left, and told the others he was going to the end of the street to distribute them.

As he went he reminded God that He used weak things and weak people. He prayed that if it was His will that they should work here that He would lead him to the right person. Then, instead of continuing to the end of the street, on an impulse he turned down an ally, and found himself at a wharf where 12 men were bringing in a fishing boat.

Hubert gave out his 12 tracts. The last man to receive one grew excited as he looked at his. He motioned Hubert into a nearby office, and picked up the phone. Hubert couldn't understand what he was saying, but in a few moments he was handed the receiver. Amazed, he heard a voice in perfect English ask why he was there. When he explained, the voice said she and her husband would like the Fishers to live there, and would find a place for them to stay. "Please come over to our house now," she finished.

So Hubert and the man, Mr. Mikami, collected the other two from the station, and were soon at his home where they met his Hawaiian-born wife. After many phone calls, Mr. Mikami announced with deep regret that there was just nowhere to rent.

As he escorted them back to the station they passed a small toolshed on stilts at the bottom of a garden.

"That's the only vacant building in Samani," he said jokingly.

"Then I'll take that," declared Hubert, with characteristic lack of "common" sense, and insisted on going up to it.

The woman of the house saw them and came to see what they were doing. On hearing the need, she said she had a room, as the teacher who had rented it had left that day. She would have hesitated to offer it to two foreigners, but if they were willing to live in a toolshed they could certainly have the room!

Mary described it in a letter home on February 25, 1953.

"After the Mikamis and Mrs. Bando, our future landlady, had consulted the almanac to make sure the day we wanted to move was a 'lucky' one, we took possession of our room. It has sliding doors on all four sides, and two of the doors open into a big cupboard, the upper part of which we use for a pantry, and the bottom holds our bedding during the day, while at night we spread it on the thick straw mats which cover the floors in Japan.

105

"We have a wood stove in the room on which, together with a little charcoal brazier, we do our cooking. Everything is very compact, so that it takes a minimum of time for housework."

"What a contrast to those huge compounds in China," she had laughed to Hubert when they moved in, and she made the best of the very cramped quarters and lack of privacy. Nevertheless Hubert wrote in June, "Mary is feeling quite tired, but still keeps going. It will buck her up quite a bit to get into our new little house in a month's time." This was actually a "couple's suite" consisting of one large room and a kitchen.

Their main work was still language study with accompanying exams, and they were very fortunate to have Mrs. Mikami as their teacher two hours a day. She was a Buddhist, of course, and they prayed repeatedly for her from the beginning, and tried to tell her of Christ.

Mary wrote home:

"During these months we've seen afresh the awful darkness of heathenism. After all our efforts to show her from the Scriptures her need of a Saviour, and lead her to the Cross where forgiveness and new life are obtained, she said it was clear. But when we then urged her to accept Christ, she said it would take time to get to that place—that really he was about the same as Buddha!"

Later Hubert mentioned that unlike Confucius, Buddha, and others, Christ's grave was empty, and for the first time Mrs. Mikami began to sense there was a difference.

She had great confidence in dreams, since some of her's had come true, and not long after this she had one in which Hubert urged her to flee, but before she could do so bombs began dropping all around her. When she told the Fishers about the dream they explained she should flee from the wrath to come on those who reject Christ. At last she was ready to acknowledge herself a sinner, and confess her need of Christ. She began reading the New Testament, and her joy was evident as she told her husband and Mrs. Bando what had happened.

Soon after Mrs. Mikami's conversion, the Fishers heard there were two other Christians in that town of 9,000; so they decided to start a Sunday afternoon service in their little room, and invite these two. One turned out to be a Roman Catholic, who never returned.

The other was a ship builder who had had contact with Methodists 35 years before, and later with Catholics, sending

106

his two daughters to one of their mission schools. One of them was now teaching in the country, and was seldom home, but the other, Noriko, had attended a Bible study while away at school, and seemed to truly believe. She bought a New Testament and read it avidly. She began to attend regularly, and later invited two others who soon accepted Christ.

Mrs. Bando came to all the meetings, and seemed to want to believe, but was stopped by what prevents most Japanese from becoming Christians: the pressure to continue worship of the ancestors from fear of their spirits' anger.

"They believe their loved ones will really suffer if they don't offer food and drink daily, and have the priest say special prayers," Mary lamented to Hubert, "and Mrs. Bando's two sons are very opposed to her becoming a Christian."

One day they met a young woman on the train from Sapporo who told them she was a Christian, and was returning to her home in Samani. She appeared very happy, and they looked forward to her help. She came twice; then they rarely saw her again. Her widowed mother had arranged her marriage to a non-Christian who didn't allow her to come.

So there were disappointments, including the father who brought along his son who had been caught stealing. The father said he had had contact with Christianity years ago, and both actually prayed to receive Christ, but never appeared again.

They found a great hindrance to Christian work in Japan was that community events of all kinds, including extra-curricular school activities, are held on Sundays, and everyone is expected to attend. Also, most of the few existing churches in Hokkaido taught a theoretical kind of Christianity, not the need for Christ as a living Saviour and Lord of one's life.

Nevertheless, in spite of the Fishers' lack of adequate language skill, after a year in Samani about a dozen people were meeting on Sundays—a remarkable result after so short a time in Japan. It made an encouraging nucleus for the two single girls who came from language school to relieve the Fishers for their much needed furlough.

Hubert had been suffering for some weeks from amoebic dysentery, and Mary had him on a liquid diet, not a very good preparation for their coming language exams in Tokyo. However he cheerily wrote to his mother of their anticipated furlough, "Living on good home food soon puts one's stomach on its feet again." They certainly had much to tell their friends and supporters of this new country which they and their fellow missionaries were now seeking to win for Christ.

Chapter 19

KINDLY ACTS,
AND GUTS TO GET THOSE BOOTS ON

When the Fishers returned a year later, the work had not progressed as much as they had hoped. The Japanese sometimes get attached to one leader, and often drop out if there is a change.

They did find Mrs. Mikami teaching a Sunday School of 50 children, and several high school students were attending services. The Fishers gradually realized the value of reaching children, and especially teenagers, in Japan. If the basics of Christianity are familiar at an early age it appears easier to withstand the pressures of ancestor worship later. Many former high school students who responded to the claims of Christ in their teens are now married to fellow Christians, and are providing the churches with much needed Christian families no longer bound by ancestor worship.

The Fishers had been back a month or so, and had just had the joy of seeing Mr. Mikami at a service for the first time, when they were asked to take charge of the new OMF Language School. This was to be in Aomori city, the northern port of the main island from which the Hokkaido ferries leave. Since all OMF work was now in Aomori prefecture or Hokkaido, it was easier to have the Language school there, too.

The Fishers viewed this new assignment with mixed feelings, but once again tried to see the plus side—helping young missionaries share as soon as possible in the work.

There was no OMF church in that area; so the Fishers attended one started by two TEAM families now on furlough, and helped there when they could. Hubert did daily house-to-house visiting in the district, leaving a tract and inviting people to come to the service, which was held in a rented kindergarten room. He never limited himself to private homes, but would enter offices, shops, or whatever dwellings he came to on a street. One day he went into a sewing school, and gave invitations to all 200 students. Only one girl, who was slightly lame, came, but she soon believed.

When a new term started, she told Hubert there was now a girl more handicapped than herself who wanted to come to the service, but it was too far for her on crutches.

That was before the Japanese motor industry produced anything but tiny taxis and three-wheel vehicles, and Hubert at once offered to take this girl, Michiko Tamura, on the back of his bike. Michiko described it nearly 30 years later.

"Mr. Fisher always came to invite me to the Sunday and evangelistic meetings. He took me on the luggage-carrier of his bicycle. I can still see his tall frame above me on the bike. He always sat me beside him in church, and like a father he opened the Bible for me, and spoke in a way which was easy for me to understand.

"My heart was very hard [because of unkindness shown her as a cripple, especially by her own father] but it gradually became soft because of his love, and I began to understand God's love in that way. The Fishers always invited Sooma-San and me to supper. We lived in the dormitory of the sewing school and his house was a mile away. Because we could not walk that far, Mr. Fisher sent a young missionary who lived with them, with a hand-pulled cart to bring us to their house. They always gave us such good meals. After supper they used to show us slides of their days in China, and sing with us. His wife was always a very gentle lady full of smiles.

"We two, while in the cart coming home one day, for the first time in our lives, felt the real warmth of human love rising up in our souls. Gradually we recognized that at the back of all their love for us was the love of God. Because they often opened the Bible and talked about it I began to have in myself a desire to read it, too. But suddenly the Fishers went off to Hokkaido. I had no chance to say goodbye, or thank them for everything, because it was so sudden . . . Six months after they left I was baptized. But the Fishers always in my eyes remained as teachers whose hearts were filled with the love of God."

Michiko went on to accomplish great things for this God she was introduced to through the Fishers.*

It seems that for the Japanese, the Fishers' many acts of simple, humble kindness, things which to us might appear trivial,

---

*Her full story appears in "Walls Are For Leaping," D.R. Pape, (OMF)

were the turning point in winning them to Christ. One woman mentions how much it meant when she was holding a baby in one hand and a heavy hymn book in the other, and Mary gently replaced it with a smaller book, saying "This will be easier."

Another writes, "When my son had an accident and was in hospital, Mrs. Fisher enquired after him, bringing a home-made cake. After that Mr. Fisher came and talked to him, for the bones in both his hands were broken, and he was passing through a time of deep despair. However, the talks Mr. Fisher had with him at that time changed the course of his life, and he was baptized soon after. Now my son has taken his place in society, and has a Christian home. I am thankful that my children and I were baptized by Mr. Fisher. In those days we were often helped and encouraged and comforted by the Scriptures. After that my two daughters were saved, and now one works at the Tokyo Christian College."

At one place, a humble act of Hubert's made a great impression on those personally involved, and on the whole church. A couple moved there who were already expecting a child before their wedding, and many were critical. The young wife became mentally unbalanced, and in an agony of guilt threw her wedding ring in the church toilet.

Hubert reasoned with her, and assured her of God's forgiveness for those who repent so she was finally calmed, and began to wish she hadn't thrown away her ring.

There were no flush toilets there, the contents of the four foot square cement container remaining for some time, to be emptied when full by the lowest class of society. Hubert took a scoop, and after filling and emptying four buckets full of the stinking mass, he saw the gold ring rise to the top, retrieved it and cleaned it. This news spread quickly. The couple were accepted by the church, and the whole spirit of the believers there was softened. Nothing could have convinced them more of Hubert's love and concern for them.

But what of the students in the Language School? How did that young fellow, probably a recent graduate from college or seminary, regard his task of dragging two crippled girls through the streets in a shabby hand-cart? No doubt the examples set by Hubert and Mary had their effect.

One student recalls his first Christmas party at the Language School. "At one point in the proceedings Hubert said, 'Now we will have a duet from Don and Dorothy Cook.' The look of utter bewilderment on both faces indicated that this was the first they knew about it, and Hubert explained, 'Always be ready for anything—that's part of the training.' "

He didn't sing particularly well himself, and was the first to admit it, but he told the students to regard this as an asset. "When you go to visit a home start singing, and when they discover they can sing better than you it will make them feel good."

Another student reported: "I had hardly got to Japan when I was asked to attend prayers for the maids at the Language School. Hubert announced: 'We will all read one verse around,' and was including me who could hardly recognize the symbols! I must confess my feelings toward him weren't the most generous at that moment, but the Lord helped me realize that whatever I was going through, He was going through it with me. Somehow I managed to stumble through, taking several times as long as anyone else. But it was part of his pattern of getting people into things as soon as possible, and not giving them time to worry about the consequences."

Hubert spoke to them on the need to *get out* and find people who could be interested in the Gospel, for very few Japanese would have courage to step into a Christian church on their own.

"The hardest part," he told them, "is to get your boots on and leave home. This is when Satan will usually try to stop you. He often says to me, 'Hubert, you're tired; go another day.' But I just pull on my boots and go." And they could see it was true.

He also told them to go out in the worst weather. "The people think you really must have something important to say, and they listen better." Since northern Japan may have snow storms at least four months of the winter, and typhoons in the summer, he had had plenty of opportunity to prove his point.

"What about barking dogs?" he was asked. "Yes, I don't like them, but don't worry." He smiled. "Once the rope tying a very fierce-sounding one broke, and instead of attacking me it ran off, so pleased to be free."

His cheerful persistence and undying enthusiasm made a lasting impression on many of his fellow workers. There was another quality which Hubert and Mary never mentioned, but which many experienced through the years. One missionary put it this way.

"The generosity of the Fishers and the light in which they

112

held possessions impressed many. Often gifts would come for them, and be passed right over to other people; so the Lord was able to trust them with a comparatively large number of personal gifts. They didn't hang on to anything more than necessary, and I understand that on occasion they completely emptied their personal account for some project at the school for missionary children, though they never had the privilege of sending any children of their own. It was quite proverbial for people to visit Aomori and be offered a suit or coat to try on, and one got the impression their home was a kind of clearing house and helping hand for all and sundry.''

In China the Fishers had often been far from fellow missionaries, especially families with children, but those in Japan really loved "Uncle Fisher." He once confided to a mother of four boys, "I wish there was someone to call me Daddy." But they never dwelt on this lack, and one Japanese mother in the Sapporo church later wrote, "Though they had no children they were very affectionate with ours. They said 'We are not lonely because we have no children. The children coming to this church are like our own. Also we have many Japanese believers who are our family.' ''

Another says, "I think they are indeed a wonderful couple. Though they had no children, they were very considerate of each other. Mr. Fisher had a very keen sense of humor, and lived a modest life. They went through many hardships where Mr. Fisher would get hurt, and Mrs. Fisher sometimes sick, but they always said 'We are thankful.' Through them I could see an ideal example of a married couple in the Lord.''

Another also mentioned Hubert's humor. Hubert once asked a young housewife if she had a child, and she answered 'We are not given one yet.' Then he said, 'We, *too*, have not been given one *yet*,' and Mr. and Mrs. Fisher were as old as Sara and Abraham then.

After just over three years at the Language School they received an urgent call to go to a promising group started recently in a mining town in Hokkaido by a missionary who now had to leave.

It must have been a hard change to make, but they gave no outward sign of this, and went to do their best. It was while there in Mikasa that one of their longstanding desires became a fact. This was for a weekly evangelistic Christian radio program to be aired in Hokkaido. OMF and others raised the money for this, which was to be the means of a real quickening of spiritual life in Hokkaido, as it was already proving to be in other parts of Japan. Some were converted directly through listening. Others who had heard it proved much easier to talk to in house-to-house visiting. Hubert always gave details of the program, and urged people to listen. Mary eventually became the treasurer for this. Later she worked and prayed for what seemed at first an impossibility because of the high cost: a series of Christian television programs for Hokkaido.

Chapter 20

TRIUMPHS AND A TRAGEDY IN SAPPORO

In their next 13 years in Japan the Fishers were asked to serve in five other towns in Hokkaido, but probably nowhere proved more satisfying and fruitful than the two periods they spent at Northern Glory church in Sapporo, the capital.

The work had begun when various university students were converted and eventually were helped to form a church, now numbering about 35, meeting in the OMF rented house. Some of the originals had now graduated and moved away, but two medical students were still there giving leadership to the group.

The Fishers were now able to reach others, bringing more maturity to the fellowship, and Mary had the joy of seeing two women's home Bible studies really grow. Space only allows for the stories of two of these women.

"I've met a Chinese lady!" Mary exclaimed excitedly to Hubert when he came home one day. "She's from Shansi. Her grandmother, an opium addict, married her to a Japanese army officer to get more money for opium. But surprisingly she was quite happy there as her husband was learning Chinese, and preferred Chinese food to Japanese—"

"Who wouldn't!" interjected Hubert. "What's her name?"

"Mrs. Takahashi. But when the war ended they had to return to Japan and live with her husband's mother in Tokyo. Mrs. T. couldn't speak any Japanese, didn't know the customs, and was made to feel a complete misfit."

"I can well imagine that!"

"It was so bad, her husband asked the bank he now worked for to transfer him to Sapporo, but even here she was out of place, and he eventually took to drink, other women, and hardly ever came home. She realized she must find a way to support herself; so went to a sewing school."

"Was it one we have visited?"

"I don't know, but she met a Miss Fukuda there, who'd also had a very unhappy life. She lost her father at a young age. A step-father with a son she couldn't get along with came into the

115

home. Then she was in hospital for years with a TB spine. These two became friends, and one day as they were having lunch together in a restaurant, Mrs. T. said things were now so bad that she'd decided this would be her last meal."

"She meant suicide?"

"Yes. So Miss Fukuda rushed to the phone, and gave Mr. T. such a tongue-lashing he came home, and treated her better for a time."

"That sounds very unusual for a Japanese woman," Hubert marvelled.

"Doesn't it! Anyway, then they were moved back to Tokyo, and the husband got worse again, and wouldn't support her. Then she got ill and went to hospital, but he wouldn't pay the bill, and the hospital wouldn't release her until it was paid. Then, what do you think happened? This is the best part!—some of the Christians at the Chinese church in Tokyo heard about her, went to see her, paid the bill, and in a short time she was converted!"

"Praise the Lord! How long ago was that?"

"About five years. She really changed then, and began to love her husband instead of hating him, and all the Chinese were praying for him. At last he attended the church, and became a Christian that day!"

"Trust the Chinese to really go after others for Christ," Hubert said with a note of nostalgia. "Well, they should be a real asset to the church here now."

"Yes, Mrs. T. said this was the last place she wanted to come when she heard they would soon be transferred again. But she finally managed to say 'even Sapporo, Lord,' just before her husband came home and said this was it."

"Why didn't she want to come here?"

"Because she was so unhappy here, and she didn't know of any churches, of course. But the Chinese told her about us, and she believes now the Lord sent her back to win Miss Fukuda to Christ, for she really saved her life before."

"She sounds a good prospect for us."

"Unfortunately they've moved to another town, but Mrs. T. plans to visit her soon."

A few days later an excited Mrs. Takahashi came to see Mary again.

"I discovered that I'd lost Miss Fukuda's address in the move. I just remembered it was in a district called In-front-of-

Temple so I went there. It was quite large, but I walked through every street, and didn't see her name up anywhere. The last bus was due to leave in 10 minutes, and I just stood in the street and prayed desperately, 'Lord, I've done all I can do. You must take over now.' Then I opened my eyes, and there was Miss Fukuda, walking towards me!''

"How wonderful!" Mary exclaimed.

"There was only time for her to tell me her family had moved back to Sapporo, and she had stayed on two days to wind up their affairs. She gave me the new address, and I told her I would visit her soon, as I had some wonderful news. Then the bus left. But since God has worked in such a marvellous way, I'm sure she'll soon be saved."

In spite of her great eagerness to see her friend, Mrs. Takahashi restrained herself until she thought the family would be fairly settled, then set off. She returned to Mary a little sadly.

"Miss Fukuda didn't seem to feel any need of Christ," she said. "Her family runs a boarding house for 27 young men, so they're very busy. But they are comfortably off now, and she is feeling well, and happier than she's ever been. So she has no time, or desire, to come to church."

"We'll keep praying for her. Don't get discouraged."

"Oh no! I had to wait four years for my husband to believe, so I'll be patient. By the way, she lives in Kotoni district. Don't you have a Bible class there?"

"Yes, please invite her to come. That won't take up so much of her time."

"That's good, we'll pray she will come to that."

Kotoni was some distance away, and Mary had been going once a month to meet with a young Christian woman who now had a baby, and couldn't get to church. Mrs. Takahashi began to attend, too, but separated from Mary on the way to call and invite Miss Fukuda. For several months she got the same reply, "I'm too busy," but on the morning of the September meeting Miss Fukuda greeted her with the words, "I'd like to go with you today to Mrs. Fisher's meeting."

Mary rejoiced to see them come in, and after she had finished what she had planned to teach the believers, she pulled out of her bag one of her old Chinese posters which clearly pictured the way of Salvation. These had generally been considered unsuitable for the sophisticated Japanese, but Mary had begun to find they really got the message across here, too; even the

117

mother of a university professor had believed after her daughter borrowed one from Mary to explain the Gospel to her.

Miss Fukuda seemed to enjoy her visit, and came the next three months. Finally, at the close of the December meeting she began to weep.

"Can the Lord possibly save such a hard-hearted, ungrateful sinner as I am?"

Mary assured her He could, and she prayed for forgiveness and new life. From that day she became one of the strongest Japanese Christians the Fishers had met. She got up at 4 a.m. on Sundays to complete her work in time to attend church. That very first New Year she told her mother she could no longer take part in the ancestor worship. She admitted one of the first things that had impressed her was that Christ could change such a hard, cruel man as Mr. Takahashi, while he confided to his wife after first meeting *her*, that the power of Christ must be great to so change the spitfire who had phoned him that day from the restaurant!

The following year the Fishers were moved to another city where Mary had a regular meeting at a Women's Reformatory, and a number accepted Christ. Mary returned to Sapporo to speak to the women there about this, and the great need for a place for prisoners to go when they were released, especially those who had recently become Christians.

One of these was a Miss Shimizu, a girl of 17 who had been deserted by her parents when she was seven, and who had constantly been in evil surroundings since.

"I'm afraid to leave this place now," she had said to Mary one day. "When I go out, how can I possibly live a life that is not sinful? I don't know anything else."

God spoke to Miss Fukuda through that, and she felt she must set up a home to receive such girls. The other Christian women became eager to help, offering bedding and clothes, and finally after much prayer, all the difficulties were overcome. Miss Shimizu came to the home, and got a job, hoping eventually to go to Bible School to train for Christian work.

The evening she received her first month's wages, Miss Fukuda gave her a mild rebuke about something, and the girl rushed away, booked into a hotel, and committed suicide with an overdose of sleeping pills.

The Christians were filled with sorrow; yet being Japanese they could understand the reasoning of this poor girl. She had suddenly felt that she could never live a life pleasing to Christ, and so, rather than bring disgrace to His Name, the honourable thing would be to leave this life with its temptations, and go quickly into the presence of the Lord she loved, before she spoiled the testimony of the church.

This tragedy was a terrible blow to Miss Fukuda, but she weathered it with the help of God and her fellow believers. Eventually she had the joy of seeing both her mother and step-father become Christians.

Meanwhile Mrs. Takahashi continued her radiant witness, always on the lookout for those in need of Christ. She proved a fellow worker after the Fishers' own hearts. She found a number of other Chinese in various places, and with Hubert and Mary's help they all became Christians.

When the Fishers had to move to other places, Mrs. T. would sometimes visit them and help in their work. The Japanese Christians admired her boldness, but said, "She can get away with it because she's Chinese. We could never do that!" In her friend Miss Fukuda, however, she found one almost as courageous as herself.

The Fishers went to Sapporo again in 1965. When they had left there before, the house was really too small for the growing congregation. Finally they had been able to build a simple church on land unexpectedly given by a visitor who heard them talking of the need. By that time they had a Japanese pastor, but he only stayed a few months.

The plan now was for the Fishers to help until a new pastor was found. As it turned out, however, they lived in the two-room apartment above the church for the next four years. The members were so happy to have them that they wanted to contribute to OMF funds, instead of paying a pastor.

One day after the morning service Hubert noticed a high school girl browsing among the library books at the back, so he went and asked her name and where she lived.

"Ishida," was the reply, and she pointed vaguely in a southeasterly direction.

Hubert prayed for her every day, but she didn't come the next week, so as soon as he could he went visiting in the southeast area. After a while he saw the name 'Ishida' over one gate.

"Here we are!" he said to himself, and with a quick prayer he opened the gate. A dog was sitting inside the open outer front door, but as soon as Hubert started up the short path it retreated to its kennel. So Hubert stepped inside the entrance, and called out the usual greeting.

Immediately a very startled woman appeared at the inner door, wondering how anyone could have approached without the dog barking. Hubert mentioned her daughter had once visited the church, and so he wondered if the mother would now like to buy her a book. He displayed what he had, and she picked out two, and asked him which would be best.

"As a matter of fact both are very good," Hubert said, "I really think it would be best to buy both."

Still bemused by the dog failing to bark, the woman purchased both, and showed Hubert a copy of *Gospel For the Millions* magazine, which a relative had recently sent.

The following Sunday a new high school student was in church, and Hubert asked her name.

"Ishida," she replied with a smile. It was a different girl from the first one; so he had evidently gone to the wrong house. But that didn't faze Hubert.

"Why not bring your mother next time?" he suggested.

The following Sunday she came with her mother and sister, and the next week the father was with them, too! Hubert regretted that he had prepared to preach on the Lord's Prayer, as it didn't seem suitable for this man, but he saw him busily taking notes during the sermon.

Later he learned Mr. Ishida went home, read through his notes, and accepted Christ. He held a high position in a mining company, and had been very arrogant and selfish at home. When his wife and daughters saw the great change in him they soon became Christians, too. This family continued strong in faith even while going through very difficult times when the mine went bankrupt. Mr. Ishida always said it was the fact of the dog not barking at Hubert which first sparked his curiosity, but possibly the Christian relative had already been praying for them.

Hubert's work was very varied in Sapporo. In addition to preaching, counselling, and visitation, there were tent campaigns in summer, and other evangelistic efforts, one resulting in the formation of a daughter church. He visited in six hospitals, taught English, and led teams of young people occasionally to distant, out-of-the-way places to help in Every Home Crusade's effort to reach every house in Japan with a visit and Christian literature.

The Fishers were still involved in promoting Christian radio programs, and their follow-up, including annual Rallies for area listeners to meet the Radio Pastor. Then came the joy and excitement of the first Christian television series. While 98 percent of Japanese homes had TV sets, it was typical that Hubert and Mary had to go for a cup of coffee in a restaurant to view the first program.

In the midst of all this happy and fruitful activity, the call came to go and relieve a missionary at a new work, and the Sapporo church very reluctantly released them. But Hubert's departure was in a way which no one could have predicted.

Chapter 21

THE SHINING FUTURE

Just as they were getting ready to leave for this new place of service, a medical check-up revealed that Mary needed surgery. Hubert therefore planned to go ahead with the move while she was in hospital. On December 1, a bitterly cold, snowy day, he was in old clothes doing the final cleaning up of their little apartment when he found he needed a small bottle stored in the low attic. He couldn't quite reach it, so rested one hand on the floor in order to stretch in further. This 'floor' was the flimsy church ceiling, however, and it collapsed beneath his weight.

Hubert recovered consciousness some time later to find himself on his back on the church platform ten feet below, and feeling very cold. In much pain, his first thought was "What can I be thankful for?"

Looking around, he saw he was in the six foot space between the pulpit and the organ, so he thanked God that he had fallen *between* them, rather than on their sharp edges. He was thankful also when he found he could move his legs, although it proved so painful he had little desire to do so!

As his mind gradually cleared, he realized it might be fatal to stay there in the freezing temperature, but what could he do? It was useless to call out, for no one was near. Somehow he must reach the phone at the church entrance. Gingerly he started to crawl and, in spite of the agonizing pain, made his way a few inches at a time over the cold floor, until finally he was beneath the phone. He reached up his hand, and found it was disconnected.

Instead of dismay, a great peace flooded his mind, and a line from a hymn rang in his ears, "We give Thee thanks, O Lord."

With prayer and a supreme effort, he gradually dragged himself upstairs to their apartment, and there telephoned the Mission doctor. She immediately sent two men who carried him downstairs on a chair, then drew him on a sleigh 200 yards across the snow to a waiting car. X-rays later showed that part of his backbone was crushed, and he had to lie in a cast for two months. But as soon as he was able to exchange this for a brace, he and Mary set off for the needy area awaiting them.

After a busy year there they went for their annual medical check-up. To their shock and horror the doctor decided that as they were both now 70, they should retire immediately. Yet only a short time before Mary had written home, "It's just a year since Hubert's accident. We are both keeping real well and praise God for His enabling."

"I can't believe it!" Hubert burst out when they left the doctor's office. "They've made a mistake this time for sure. God promised after my breakdown in '33 that He would add those years on the end of my ministry.

Mary agreed, but sadly they had to accept the Mission decision. Hubert could see no plus in this unwelcome situation for quite a while, and it was Mary who wrote to their supporters after their return to Canada:

"Some of you will be surprised to see our change of address . . . We were in good health, and had hoped for another two years before retirement . . . but God has enabled us to take this decision as from Him. We have left part of our hearts behind, and the love and affection shown at the six farewells for us will remain a happy memory.

"God has enabled us to see many come to know Him during our 20 years in Japan. Some are in the Lord's work now, both in Japan, and in various mission fields; young couples are establishing Christian homes; others preparing in Bible School or Seminary for future ministry; through special ministries such as radio, TV, film evangelism, coffee shop evangelism, and camps, etc. the Gospel continues to go out, and believers are becoming more aggressive in their personal witness. Pray this may continue."

Hubert's part of the letter was more negative. He didn't refer to their coming home at all, but instead gave a vivid picture of unmet needs in Japan, ending with a visit he had paid to a woman who seemed to be seeking. "I didn't go back—I wonder if a missionary ever will? What a harvest is being reaped by the devil because *we* do not go and reap for Christ!"

Their retirement still seemed to him one big, miserable minus. They spent their first month back in Canada visiting various relatives of Mary's. On entering the room in one of these homes Hubert noticed a Christian calendar on the wall, and in desperation suddenly prayed that God would give him direction from it for their future. He couldn't forget God's assurance in his earlier breakdown that He would add years of service at the end of his life. He had fully expected these to be in Japan, hence his belief that leaving there was a terrible mistake.

As he crossed the room to read the calendar he saw it had just two verses on it. The first went right to his heart. "I will turn the curse into a blessing." Leaving Japan had indeed been a horrible minus, yet here was God promising a blessing from it! What a comfort that was, and all his doubts were immediately dissolved.

The second verse also had a clear message. "Mind not high things, but condescend to men of low estate." Joyfully Hubert took that to be the guiding principle for the remainder of his life, and immediately set about finding ways to put it into practice.

They settled in a block of retirement apartments in Vancouver, and at this time of writing Mary, now 84, still helps to care for other residents in need, and does hospital visitation. God also had a joyful surprise for them in that city, the opportunity to help in a Mandarin-speaking Chinese church. Mary taught a teenage Sunday School class, and runs a women's meeting, while Hubert, as associate pastor preached once a month, conducted any weddings or funerals, and had more than doubled attendance at the Youth Fellowship. They both did a lot of walking, and no one could guess their age.

The Chinese work indeed proved to be the "blessing" of the verse on the calendar, but Hubert did not forget the second verse. Soon he offered his services to the Union Gospel Mission which has a wide ministry to various needs, but especially to those whose way of life has led to Skid Row. At first Hubert also helped in boarding ships in the harbor, carrying suitcases filled with Christian literature in many languages for sailors from all over the world, but after some years had to confine himself to land-based activities. He worked in the Mission's Counselling room two afternoons a week, when he might see from two to twenty men coming in to share their problems over tea and a doughnut. He also frequently walked in the parks, getting into conversation with people, and giving out tracts and invitations to the meetings. But his long practice of door-to-door visitation also claimed much of his time, though this now included cheap hotels and common lodging houses catering to impoverished Indians, and others in difficulties through drink or drugs, or teenagers running away from home.

One day he met an alcoholic Irishman who threatened him with a knife. Another time he went into a room where a burly Irish fellow was sitting on his bed drinking. He listened to Hubert for a while, but with frequent tipping of the bottle.

"Suddenly he got up," Hubert reported later, "put one big hand on my head, and the other on my throat. 'I'll show you how to kill a man using only your hands,' he said. I was relieved when the lesson was over! In the next hotel I found a young Christian man. He informed me that the people in the place I had just come from were a very bad bunch. I reminded him that Christ had died for them, too." It was this conviction which still kept Hubert seeking the helpless, the hopeless, or anyone without Christ.

Some of these seemed so hopeless, or resistant to the Gospel, that even Hubert was occasionally tempted to give up on them. He wrote to his prayer partners about one of them.

On Monday afternoons Hubert held a meeting at the Union Gospel Mission, which incidentally had grown from about a dozen when it started in 1980 to over 100 men drawn by Hubert's clear, simple, loving presentation of the Gospel, illustrated by many examples from his life on the railway, or in China and Japan. Hubert usually got there early to sort through the tract supply, and on one particular Monday he took off his watch, so he would be reminded of the time of the meeting. He remembered the meeting, but forgot to put his watch on again. On his return the watch was gone, for many men passed the table and stopped to look at the literature.

The watch was a special railwayman's one, and had been given Hubert by the daughter of its owner on her father's death. Mary and Hubert prayed earnestly that it might be returned, but when he went to the Mission on Wednesday there was no word of it, nor did he hear anything of it the following week. Most people would have given up praying then, but not Hubert.

When he entered the Mission on the tenth day after his loss he saw two men who were trying to break off drugs; so he went over and chatted with them. When he was about to move on, one of them handed Hubert his watch, saying a man called "C" had given it to him two days ago.

"C" was an alcoholic they had worked with for several years, but he had had so many lapses they had almost decided he wasn't worth bothering with any more. For Hubert now it wasn't just a matter of being thankful to get his property back. He said, "I felt that by the Lord using him to give my watch back He was telling me not to give up on him."

That same month, another incident in Hubert's life indicated the Lord's loving care. An elderly tenant whom Hubert was helping to move out of his apartment, gave him a few things he didn't want to take with him. One of these was a good, almost new right shoe! It fitted Hubert perfectly, but of what use was one shoe? A week later he was doing visitation in another area, and had just missed a bus back. To pass the time he walked down the street, and happened to see the Salvation Army Thrift Shop. On a shelf in front were about a dozen left shoes, one of which looked remarkably like his right one. He enquired about buying the pair, and the helper searched everywhere, finding the mates of all the shoes except the one he wanted. So Hubert joyfully took the one, and ended up with a good pair of shoes. Thus the Lord continued to bless Hubert and Mary in special little ways as they served him with all their hearts.

Evidence of the Fishers' sensitivity to God's leading can be seen in their ability to adjust their methods of evangelism to suit the needs of the people they sought to reach. In Japan, where culture and circumstances were very different from China where they had had such good response, the esteem with which they were held is unmistakable. A Christian in Sapporo wrote, "Many foreigners have been recognized for their service to Japan, but I think Mr. and Mrs. Fisher are worthy of a special heavenly reward." Not only Japanese, but many others would agree, and have no doubt that a warm "Well done!" will greet them from their welcoming Lord.

There are perhaps few men who have experienced so clearly God's guidance and power in perplexing situations big and small, or who have been so quick to obey. Hubert's courage in the face of many dangers in China, and the darkest corners of Vancouver, have been a wonder and encouragement to other and younger men. Certainly there are few people in our affluent and materialistic society who have so consistently held to such a simple lifestyle as Hubert and Mary Fisher. Nor have many modelled more closely the life and relationship to the Lord which is portrayed in the following hymn:

> O Master let me walk with Thee
> In lowly paths of service free,

Tell me Thy secret, help me bear
The strain of toil, the fret of care.

Help me the slow of heart to move
By some clear winning word of love.
Teach me the wayward feet to stay
And guide them in the heavenward way.

In hope that sends a shining ray
Far down the future's broadening way.
In peace that only Thou canst give
With Thee, O Master, let me live.

Washington Gladden
1879

POSTSCRIPT

This manuscript was completed soon after the incidents of the watch and shoe. Hubert continued "putting his boots on" and going out to fish for men and lead them to Christ until May 16 when he began experiencing pain around a rib which had been injured in a fall the previous year. In June it was diagnosed as inoperable cancer. Now in intense pain, Hubert was able to rejoice that this agonizing minus meant the exceeding joy of soon being in Christ's presence. He was able clearly to testify to this to all who attended him in the hosptial, and this joy became a reality on July 1st, 1985, in his 84th year.

He had previously chosen as the text for his memorial service Psalm 37:23, which begins "The steps of a good man are ordered by the Lord." He wanted all to know that this painful illness was no mistake, but allowed by a loving Father, and a clear evangelistic message was given at the service of how man becomes good—through faith in the crucified Savior.

Perhaps the most moving part of the service was the singing of the hymn "Face to face with Christ my Savior," in both Chinese and English, by the Mandarin Church Choir. Hubert is now enjoying that experience. Because of his enthusiastic, loving and courageous ministry, countless Chinese, Japanese and Canadians whom he has introduced to Christ over more than 60 years as God's strongly motivated fisher of men, will be able to share his joy.